D1569653

SHADOW DANCER

A John Treehorn Mystery

Dinah Miller

New York Productions, LLC
P. O. Box 175
Churubusco, New York 12923

Shadow Dancer: A John Treehorn Mystery is a work of fiction. Names, characters, places, and incidents are either the product of the author's imagination or are used fictitiously. Any resemblance to actual persons, living or dead, events, or locales is entirely coincidental.

ISBN 978-0-9979826-0-2

Printed in the United States of America

Cover Artwork by Leonie Cheetham
https://www.facebook.com/leoniecheethamart

www.dinahmiller.com (Books and merchandise.)

www.facebook.com/SpecialAgentJohnTreehorn/

To Dane

A victim never forgets.

FBI Special Agent John Treehorn

Chapter One

The Arizona sunrise shadow danced along the sandstone walls of the ravine until it touched the flat stone. A gravestone which only two men ever knew existed: the one buried beneath, and the one who had buried him... alive.

FBI Headquarters, Washington, DC - Present Day

Special Agent John Treehorn entered the heavy glass doors of the J. Edgar Hoover Building at the Federal Bureau of Investigation carrying two large coffees. He was taller than most Navajos, and at age thirty-five, was one of the most decorated agents in the Washington bureau. He was six foot in height, lean with a jet-black regulation, government FBI haircut. The majority of Native Americans have brown eyes, but this man did not. He had brown-blue heterochromic eyes: brown on the outer rims, blue on the inner part. When this man examined you, it conveyed to all that he's different. Men stepped aside when he entered the elevator. They recognized an alpha male, not one molded by a golden spoon, but one

1

born with its faceted genes. As he leaned against the rear wall of the elevator, Treehorn surveyed the occupants of the confined space with his ingrained law-enforcement training. The three men ignored him, whereas the three women weren't shy. They admired his height, the breadth of his shoulders beneath the fine-cut dark suit, and his tanned complexion, while they envied the woman who wore the matching wedding ring.

Treehorn greeted his trusted administrator as he entered his office. The woman was already in need of more coffee. She smiled as he handed her two large containers. Her smile always brightened his day, "Good morning, Abby."

She inhaled her morning elixir, "Good morning. Boss wants to see you, and your reports are on your desk. Good work, John."

"Thanks."

As Treehorn passed Abby, he gave a professional nod to the new transfer agent, Rebecca Bridges. As he walked away from the reception area, her eyes followed his back.

Abby then caught her gaze. "Not going to happen," she said to the newcomer with a sympathetic smile.

Rebecca sighed, "I know. What's his count?"

"Fifty-six," Abby answered as she thought of the cases and families her favorite agent had helped.

"Well, at least he's good at something." The girl's humor made Abby chuckle.

"Oh, I think he's good at many things," said Abby, as she watched Treehorn's long, muscular legs travel the corridor toward his supervisor's office. Younger agents moved aside as he walked past. Abby gave a hormonal sigh and went to prepare tea for the woman who waited in the director's office for answers on a cold case.

Treehorn knocked on the open door of FBI District Supervisor Leo Mancuso's office who motioned for his agent to enter. His boss wasn't alone. An older, designer-dressed woman, clutching a tissue, sat in one of the oak gray-blue upholstered chairs. Her eyes were red and swollen from crying, but at that moment they were dry.

"Eliza Hemingford, meet Special Agent John Treehorn," Mancuso made the introductions.

Treehorn shook a soft, late-fifties feminine hand. He observed she wore a single, gold wedding band on her ring finger.

"Thank you for taking the time to meet with me, Mr. Treehorn." She sounded weak and tired. Someone or something had aged this woman.

Mancuso handed Treehorn a folder. "I want you to reopen this cold case. Fifteen years ago, a prep-school employee and the four boys he supervised disappeared during a camping trip. The boys were found the next day, but the man is still missing."

Treehorn perused the file, "Your relation to the case?" he asked.

"My son, Edward, was one of the students," Eliza answered.

"She has new information on a crime with this case," Mancuso said, standing to shake her hand, "I'll let her discuss it with you in private."

Treehorn nodded and masked his curiosity.

"Let's hope we can find who is responsible and take action to rectify the situation. Thank you for coming forward."

"Thank you, Mr. Mancuso." She stood and shook his hand.

Mancuso watched his agent assist this woman who was worn down by her misery. He assigned his best man, with personal ties connected to the area where the boys had camped and disappeared. If anyone could solve this cold case, which occurred on the Navajo Reservation, it would be his Navajo agent.

Treehorn and Eliza walked in silence for the distance to the agent's office. Mancuso's office was on the sunny side of the building, so it shone with the morning light, while Treehorn's office sat on the opposite side of the floor, next to the storeroom. While Mancuso's office had two chairs for visitors and an extra couch for relaxing, there was room for only a wooden chair in Treehorn's cubbyhole. It was a sparse, neat office and somehow he had found the room for two picturesque, framed photographs of the Grand Canyon and Monument Valley. Next to those were his University of Arizona Law Degree and two of his Distinguished Merit awards. The others were filling up the bottom of his filing cabinet.

Eliza admired the photographs, "Where are you from, Mr. Treehorn?"

"I was born and raised on the Navajo Indian Reservation," Treehorn answered and offered no further personal details. He reached for his writing pad and pencil.

"I'm from New York. Edwin was too. We were never familiar with the West, but this trip would be a big eye-opener for Edward," Eliza said as she started her son's journey.

"What's the new information?" The agent asked.

Eliza searched for the right words to fit the circumstance. Treehorn examined her with a trained eye. No amount of makeup could soften the years of suffering etched on her face.

She gathered strength from her soul and whispered, "My son was raped. I want you to find out who committed this horrific crime."

Treehorn re-examined the file. "There's no mention of it. The papers state that this is a missing person case." The agent wondered why his supervisor had assigned him to investigate a crime where the statute of limitations had expired long ago.

"My husband, Edwin, died a week ago. He never reported it to the authorities and never told me," Eliza added.

"I'm sorry," the agent had lost count of the number of investigations where victims were reluctant to discuss their attacks, especially the male sexual assaults.

Eliza sighed with her sorrow, "Cancer took my husband too soon, but he left me a detailed note with an apology. He was just too ashamed to report it."

Treehorn studied her face and understood the difficulty she faced. "Would you like something to drink? Tea or water?" It would give her time to compose herself.

"I appreciate that Mr., sorry, Agent Treehorn. I would love some plain tea. Thank you."

Treehorn picked up one of the little china cups from the tray and poured the hot liquid. He set it near her, since it appeared that her hand wasn't steady enough to hold the delicate cup. He made a mental note to thank Abby for her kindness. He examined the few pages in the folder while she sipped her drink. It included an enlargement of a New York State driver's license photo labeled Jeff Hodges who was a smiling white male age forty-five with a Manhattan address.

"Jeff Hodges was the group leader and driver?" Treehorn asked as he examined the other documents.

"Yes," Eliza responded.

The next page showed four photos of fifteen-year-old boys with their names attached. He read aloud: "Edward Hemingford, Andy Foster, Frank Pierce, and Jack Garner."

"Our son, Edward, is an only child. Years ago, we sent our normal, intelligent kid on a wonderful and educational trip..." She paused, "...and then, upon his return, we watched helplessly as he spiraled downhill with drug abuse and multiple suicide attempts." She paused again and took a breath. She stared at nothing and then composed herself. "He celebrated his thirtieth birthday, yesterday, in the hospital."

"Is he still an inpatient?" Treehorn asked.

"Yes, at Bellingham Psychiatric Hospital."

"All right. I'd like to interview him, and I'd prefer to do that with you present. Could you accompany me there, now?" Treehorn asked.

Eliza nodded, "Yes, my chauffeur can drive us."

"Thank you for the offer, but I'll meet you there."

Bellingham Psychiatric Hospital

The psychiatric hospital was an old, cold-looking, monstrosity of dark-red brick that reminded Treehorn of a prison more than a hospital. He signed his weapon into a secured cabinet, as required by law. He walked with Eliza toward a pair of locked security doors which were guarded by a mental health aide. The chatter of patients' voices echoed into the hallway. The white-clad orderly unlocked the doors leading to the psychiatric ward.

"Good morning, Mrs. Hemingford," the man greeted her and nodded to Agent Treehorn.

"Good morning, Michael," she smiled.

"Edward's in the activity room. He's drawing." The orderly knew his routine.

"Is he having a bad day?" Eliza didn't expect good news.

"He's having a normal day," Michael replied. The aide closed the old metal door. The clanging echoed down the hallway. As the key turned and secured the lock, its security reminded Treehorn that this was a hospital for tortured minds, not the criminally insane, but both felt like a prison.

"I'll let the doctor know you've arrived."

"Thank you, Michael."

Treehorn accompanied Eliza into the activity room. They both stopped and observed the activities. There were five psychiatric patients present with a couple aides. Patients were dressed in jeans and t-shirts. The staff members wore standard white uniforms. A couple of patients directly ahead watched a comedy television show while others, over to the right, painted with bright, primary colors, the tempera paints favored by kindergartners.

"There's Edward," Eliza pointed to a man who stood in the corner at a chalkboard. Treehorn spotted her disheveled son with his long, brown hair and shaggy beard. The male appeared older than his thirty years. The agent watched as the patient obsessively focused on the black chalkboard. His hand repeatedly struck the slate with a large piece of chalk. Tap, tap, tap. He kept repeating the rhythm of a drum playing its own tune.

Dr. Virginia Fields, a clinical psychiatrist dressed in a stylish white coat, stepped out from her glass-enclosed office. At just five feet, she displayed no need for high heels. It was clear that her height was neither linked to her level of experience nor her confidence. Her pale skin gave away that she spent too many hours indoors. Her blue eyes looked over Treehorn with insight. She made it clear, before they even met, he would get professional courtesy from her, but nothing more.

Eliza Hemingford introduced her, "Dr. Fields, this is FBI Special Agent John Treehorn."

"Thank you for seeing us on such short notice." Treehorn shook her hand.

"It's not a problem. Come into my office where we can

talk in private."

Everyone settled in chairs next to a desk stacked with files. Treehorn looked around and took things in.

At fifty, Dr. Fields appeared at the top of her game. On the wall behind her were the diplomas showing she was a graduate of Georgetown and Johns Hopkins.

Eliza addressed a confidentiality issue, "As Edward's legal guardian, I signed for Agent Treehorn to have full access to his medical records to assist him in this investigation."

Dr. Fields nodded at this and turned to the Fed. "Thank you, Agent Treehorn, for reopening this case. Eliza called and informed me of her meeting with your agency today. After we spoke, I pulled all of Edward's records." The psychiatrist glanced at the stacked files on her desk and offered her clinical version of his history with a diagnosis. "This is Edward's fifth in-patient hospitalization at Bellingham, but the first since I joined the team."

"Have all of his admissions been after the assault during his trip West?" Treehorn again silently questioned why his supervisor had ordered this case reopened.

"Yes, and near the anniversary of it, too," Dr. Fields confirmed. "We have definitively concluded that the assault was the trigger for his crisis. He had no documented psychiatric history prior to the trip."

"Are there any details in the files about his assault?" Treehorn asked as he took notes.

"No. Mrs. Hemingford notified us, and I searched the records for it," Dr. Fields added. "I'm not surprised. Many men refuse to discuss assaults and bury the incidents."

Eliza pursed her lips in distress, "Can you help him now that you know, Doctor?"

"I hope so, but I can't make any promises." Dr. Fields examined a document, "I'll get them sent to your office as soon as we're done here. Now, let me tell you about Edward. He is a thirty-year-old man with a history of suicidal ideation and delusions. He is fixed on two repeating images: one, he carved into his chest and the second, he repeatedly draws. We have been at a loss as to what they mean, if anything."

"Do you have a photo of his chest carving?" Treehorn wanted a copy for the file.

The psychiatrist handed one across the desk to him. "Here's the image we've photographed from his body. Edward will sit for hours in front of a mirror, watching it watch him."

The agent examined the photograph. The image was

likely carved with a dull knife due to its rough puckered edges. The scars covered Edward's chest and abdomen. On top was a half circle with circles around his nipples, making them look like eyes. The bottom half had one solid line with ten lines sliced straight down from it. The Indian recognized the symbol, what it represented, and broke into a sweat.

"What is it, Agent Treehorn?" Dr. Fields asked as she interrupted his thoughts.

"This is a Navajo Indian gravestone marker," he informed both women.

"Why would Edward carve one of those on his body?" Eliza's anxious voice whispered.

"I can't speculate," Treehorn wondered if Edward had knowledge of where a body could be buried. The agent returned the picture to Dr. Fields, "What's the other image?"

"He called it Shadow Dancer and claims it took his soul." The psychiatrist removed the image from the file.

Treehorn felt faint as the blood drained from his face. His eyes fixed on the wall, but his mind traveled elsewhere.

Navajo Indian Reservation - Antelope Ravine - 15 years earlier

13

In the desert land where little rain falls, the sandstone cliffs are eroded from the fast-moving torrents of water that drench them during the Arizona monsoon season. There are canyons and ravines that few white men have seen to this day. A campfire burns brightly on the red soil under a black night sky. The beat of an Indian drum fills the ravine. Out of the shadows, a Native American dancer emerges. Feathers cover his body to mimic a great burning fire. The dancer chants in Navajo as he beats his drum. The Shadow Dancer's image grows larger on the sandstone wall to a gigantic size. Over the beating of the drum, a woman's screams echo against the walls but soon die away. The drums continue their boom, boom, boom... The Shadow Dancer is here.

The agent stood and walked out of the doctor's office without an explanation.

The two women looked at each other with raised eyebrows as they watched his hasty departure, then both shrugged their shoulders in confusion.

Treehorn approached Edward and his chalkboard.

Dr. Fields and Eliza raced to catch up with the agent.

The taps of chalk… the beat of the drum… tap, tap,

14

tap... boom, boom, boom. The two opposing sounds reverberated in Treehorn's head. Shadows moved against a canyon wall in a ghost-like manner in his mind.

Edward continued to tap the black slate. Dot by dot, a nightmare emerged. Two big eyes in a dark mask, feathers, and flames covered the board.

Eliza gasped, and her eyes filled with tears of horror.

Treehorn staggered against the wall. His body went numb from the top of his head to the bottom of his soles. Blackness threatened to engulf him as he struggled to fill his lungs. He grabbed the nearest chair and fell into it. He stared at the floor until the dizziness passed. When his breathing returned to normal, he removed his phone and snapped a picture of the chalked image.

Dr. Fields watched the agent's shock and recovery. As she gauged his response to the chalkboard, the surprise on her face betrayed her professionalism and, at the same time, revealed genuine concern. This man lived with a horror.

Treehorn spotted the doctor looking at him in a clinical manner, not the come-hither way he got all the time from other women. It unnerved him for a moment. He avoided eye contact with her, as if it would block her view into his mind, and he sought privacy to contact his supervisor. "Excuse me."

The two women watched as he removed his telephone and walked a few steps away for privacy.

Treehorn telephoned Mancuso with this development. A serious incident had occurred on the Land of his People.

His boss answered on the first ring, "Mancuso."

"Treehorn here, I know who committed this crime," the agent stated as he loosened his necktie.

Edward continued his tapping, oblivious to all.

"Who?" Mancuso checked the clock.

Treehorn hesitated, "He's called Shadow Dancer, and he lives on the Navajo Indian Reservation."

"Is he one of your myths?" Mancuso responded.

"Myth to some, real to others, but myths don't commit crimes, people do." Treehorn's body tingled as his blood coursed through it, making him feel uneasy.

Mancuso examined his agent's caseload, closure rate, and merit awards. He couldn't deny that Treehorn was one of his best agents, that he followed the FBI playbook, and he didn't flaunt his half-breed American Indian status when it might have suited him. The trouble that Mancuso had with this agent was twofold. One, the director could never read him. Two, Treehorn believed in myths.

Treehorn could tell by the long silence over the phone that Mancuso was having doubts. Yet, he knew that, in the end, his boss would let him do the one thing he excelled at: his job.

"Interview the victim's wife and the two local boys. See if they remember any new facts, not myths, that will solve this case," Mancuso instructed.

Treehorn knew when to follow orders. "Yes, sir."

"Then, I'll decide how to proceed." Mancuso ended the call with the last word, as always.

The agent knew that Mancuso trusted him to do his job and that he would achieve results. He made his supervisor look good to the one person who mattered most: FBI Director, Andrew Mason.

Edward continued his chalk tapping while his mother observed her son with sad, tired eyes.

Treehorn eyed the women who wanted answers on a professional level and personal level. "I promise you we'll do our best to help Edward find peace," The man stated with

17

conviction.

Dr. Fields shook his hand. "Thank you, Agent Treehorn. If I find any information to assist in this investigation, I'll forward it to you immediately."

"Thank you for helping my son," Eliza added. "I appreciate it more than I can express."

The agent wondered whether any answers he found would remove the sadness that filled this mother's eyes or add to it.

Chapter Two

Jeff Hodges' wife, Cynthia, lived in a picturesque farmhouse on a knoll overlooking Columbia County, southeast of Albany. She had moved there from the city after her husband's disappearance to be closer to her own family. It was a peaceful place to raise a child.

Agent Treehorn sat in her kitchen. It had a rustic-feeling coziness. The kitchen overlooked an expanse of grass and a gravel driveway that sloped to the road.

She poured coffee for Treehorn and herself.

"We've received a new lead in the investigation, so we've reopened it. What can you remember about your husband in the events that led up to his disappearance?"

Treehorn sipped his drink.

"Here's our wedding photo, Agent Treehorn. Let me tell you about the wonderful man I married."

Treehorn examined the image that showed a smiling couple on their special day.

"We married after I graduated from art school. It was a perfect profession for us to raise a family. I could be a stay-at-home mom, take care of our child, and still do my artwork."

Treehorn viewed the group photographs on the windowsill. Cynthia handed him a picture of Jeff, herself, and their infant. It captured a joyous moment.

"That's our son, David. He was six months old when Jeff departed on the trip," Cynthia's lips showed a ghost of a smile as she looked at her baby.

"How would you describe your marriage?" Treehorn replaced the frame on the ledge.

If Cynthia was offended by the interrogation, she didn't show it. "We had a loving, committed relationship. Jeff was accused of abandoning us and he wasn't here to defend himself."

"The police assumed your husband stole the vehicle and ran off with another woman," The agent read the notes from the file.

"Agent Treehorn, I suffered two miscarriages before the birth of our son. He was there, by my side, every minute for me. He was faithful and a good man. I don't believe he ever even glanced at another female."

Treehorn believed her because he knew men like Jeff Hodges did exist. "Why would they accuse Jeff of abandoning you?" Treehorn knew the liability issue.

This question offended Cynthia. "The prep school wants you to believe that."

"Why?" Treehorn grilled.

"Why?" Cynthia's tone became testy, not at Treehorn's questions, but at the feelings she relived from the time her spouse went missing. "My husband worked ten years for that rich kid's snob school. It removed their responsibility. It was easier for them to imply he disappeared with a woman. The only problem was they had no concrete evidence to back up their theory."

"What happened when he didn't reappear?" Treehorn guessed the outcome.

"They waited a week then fired him. The next day they evicted us out of their housing program," Cynthia answered as she reached for more tissues.

"I'm sorry," Treehorn sympathized.

"The life insurance company refused to pay his multi-million-dollar policy. They said, 'Show us the body and we'll show you the money.' We lost everything," Cynthia voiced her grief.

"That's a standard operating procedure for financial

companies." Treehorn observed it time after time in his investigations but they expedited payment when the body appeared. He made sure of it.

"My lawyer instructed me to have Jeff declared dead, so I could sue the insurance company, but I refused," Cynthia voiced her bitterness.

"Why?" Treehorn saw the sorrow on the woman's face.

"I needed to believe my husband was still alive when I looked in our son's eyes," Cynthia replied as she stared at her family photo.

"Was there anything about this excursion that was different?" The agent examined the itinerary he obtained.

"I'll be honest, I felt something bad would occur on that trip and it made me anxious," Cynthia stated.

Treehorn focused on her intuition, "Go on."

"My premonition came true," Cynthia wiped the tears from her eyes. "I begged him not to go. I knew he wouldn't return, but he refused."

"Is there any information you remember now that wasn't reported years earlier?" Treehorn hoped for a new clue.

"No, but you can ask the Navajo Nation Police and the FBI field office why they didn't do a thorough investigation into my husband's disappearance," she said. "I know a crime was committed and someone failed to do their job."

Treehorn finished his coffee and stood up. "I'm sorry this was difficult, and I can't imagine the life you've had without your husband. I promise you, our agents will go over this case with a fine-tooth comb regardless how long it takes. You and your son deserve answers."

"Thank you, Agent Treehorn, but we both know those rich, prep-school boys remember what happened to my husband on that trip, and they're not talking," Cynthia wiped her tears.

The agent asked himself the same question as he returned to DC on the commuter flight.

The Law Firm of Pierce, Long, & Langley - Washington, DC

Entering the lobby of one of the most prestigious law firms in Washington, DC, Agent Treehorn presented his identification to the receptionist behind a mahogany desk. As soon as he signed the ledger, a phone buzzed, and the young woman answered it.

"Agent Treehorn, Mr. Pierce will see you now." The

woman pointed to a closed door.

The agent watched as it opened where another female assistant waited to usher him into the sacrosanct hallway to the partners' offices. This hallway impressed: It was wide enough for a small car to drive through without even grazing the side. Tables holding vases with fresh-cut flowers were stationed between every other oak-paneled office door with a gleaming brass nameplate. The plush, navy blue carpets didn't show the least amount of wear, while framed original artwork worth millions adorned the walls. An interior decorator had earned his or her high six-figure fee and letters of recommendation for this job. Treehorn allowed himself the tiniest bit of self-indulgence to judge that this was the world of the white man's white man.

The woman stopped in front of the last office door on the right which led into an oak-paneled office.

Treehorn entered. A vintage Stickley oak desk in front of a window provided a direct view of both the mall and the Washington Monument. Dozens of framed diplomas, certificates, honors, and awards were strategically placed for any incoming set of eyes. Every part of the room reinforced the office's message: Power & Prestige.

The woman silently closed the door behind him.

Four well-groomed, blue-eyed Ivy League lawyers in tailored dark blue suits watched Treehorn enter their sacred establishment. The agent hadn't expected a warm welcome and he wasn't disappointed. Donovan Pierce, the epitome of silver-haired legal royalty, stood at the side of his desk, whispering to Congressman Peter Garner, a slick-haired politician with a reputation for throwing his weight around behind closed doors. Several feet away, deferential to the old men in the room, stood their sons: Frank Pierce and Jack Garner, both thirty, consumed with their sense of entitlement and serious affluenza. Arrogance flowed from their pores like sweat at the nearest country club. Treehorn had observed it many times. No one stepped forward to offer a handshake. No greeting. Their body language spoke volumes, and the man suspected: they had something to hide. "FBI Special Agent John Treehorn, Washington division," he stated, in his most professional voice. He took his time showing his badge and photo ID to each man.

"Have a seat," Pierce said curtly, heading for his own. He motioned with his hand in Garner's direction,

"Congressman Peter Garner."

The politician pointed to the young men, "My son, Jack, on your right."

Treehorn made a quick mental note: average height and build, conservatively neat, nodded, and made brief eye contact.

Pierce introduced his own, "My son, Frank."

The agent acknowledged him.

A lean, trim man nodded, and then became fascinated with Treehorn's tie pin.

"Take a seat," Pierce ordered, and it was time to conduct business. No refreshments were offered.

The agent assessed the dynamics at play in their domain as he sat in the only unclaimed chair. "I asked to speak to your sons," Treehorn reiterated as he voiced his simple request.

Pierce spoke, "We're busy men, Agent Treehorn. The boys gave their statements at the time of the incident. The group leader, Jeff Hodges, abandoned them."

"Are you representing them as their attorney?" Treehorn queried.

"Do they need representation?" slick lawyer Pierce responded.

Four pairs of lawyers' eyes fixed on Treehorn.

He ignored the fathers and instead focused on Frank Pierce and Jack Garner. After a few studied moments, he opened his file and removed the police report. Treehorn focused on Jack Garner. "I want to hear what happened, from you."

The young man glanced at his father for permission to speak.

The congressman made a barely perceptible nod.

"We went on a school camping trip, Agent Treehorn. The plane landed in Phoenix. Jeff signed for the rental van. He drove us to parks and tourist attractions," Jack detailed the travel itinerary.

Treehorn watched Frank Pierce and his sudden fascination with his hand-stitched, leather wingtips that no FBI agent could afford or wear to chase down a criminal. "Where did you camp the last night?" Treehorn grilled.

"San-san-sandstone, Sandstone Cliffs, near Ca-Ca-Canyon de Chelly," Jack's arrogance vanished as his stutter emerged.

The climate-controlled room wasn't keeping up with Frank's sudden bout of sweat. His face became paler with every word Jack spoke.

"What happened?" Treehorn prodded.

"We fe-fe-fell asleep. In the morning we were ne-ne-near a highway. No Hodges, no vehicle." Jack's timeline missed a lot of time.

"Were you under the influence of alcohol or drugs?" The agent asked.

"Agent Treehorn!" Pierce interrupted.

Treehorn ignored Jack's father and prompted, "Answer the question."

Jack looked to his father and, by the look, his legal advisor, too. "We had a bottle of liquor. I called my father and his plane brought us home,"

Yes, thought Treehorn, the first call is always to Daddy who sends the private jet. "Were you taken to the hospital for drug tests?" Treehorn interrogated.

"The boys were examined by my personal physician," Pierce interjected. "They were treated for dehydration."

Treehorn knew his next question wouldn't be answered by any attorney. "Are there any details you remember now that weren't in the original police report?" Treehorn asked as he pointed to the document he held.

Jack and Frank eyed each other, shaking their heads as if they had scripted the whole interview in advance. Frank's facial hue had settled back into its normal shade of white and rich. "No," they replied, simultaneously.

Choreographed!

Treehorn refused to let up, "Not a single detail?"

"Asked and answered, Agent Treehorn," the congressman interjected.

"I would like a copy of the medical report. It's not in the file," Treehorn requested.

"The boys suffered from dehydration," Pierce repeated.

"Is your fax broken?" Treehorn asked with the driving force of a gavel in a courtroom.

Four lawyers had misjudged their adversary. They accepted in their legal minds that FBI Special Agent John Treehorn had tied this round. He would leave only with a supposition, but they knew his type. He would return.

"I'll have the report sent to you," Pierce conceded.

Treehorn and the older men stood.

The sons remained seated and avoided eye contact with the Fed.

Turning to Congressman Garner, Treehorn nailed them,

"Your son's statement sounds like a sanitized police report."

Pierce cut in, "We're done here and that's the lawyer speaking."

Proffering the congressman his business card Treehorn raised his hand to shake the man's.

The Congressman's sweaty palm matched his sweaty face.

The office door opened and the assistant, who must have waited outside, moved to escort the agent out.

"I'll be in touch," Treehorn uttered the foregone conclusion.

As he exited The Law Firm of Pierce, Long, & Langley, Treehorn called his supervisor on his direct line.

"Mancuso."

"Treehorn here. I finished with the lawyers. What do you have when a lawyer's accounting of a story reads like a police report?"

"We assume they have something to hide. Fly out to the Navajo Reservation and lead the investigation," Mancuso ordered.

"Agent Shelly works their field office and he's capable

of supervising this," Treehorn countered.

"I've ordered you to go," Mancuso directed.

"I have four open files on my desk, sir," Treehorn reminded him and resisted the assignment.

"They're cold. They'll wait!" Mancuso's patience disappeared.

"This is a cold case, too. I can coordinate the investigation here, while Agent Shelly keeps me posted from the reservation."

"I'm ordering you." Mancuso was the boss and expected his orders to be followed, but Treehorn had determination.

"Sir." The agent stood firm.

"Do you have trouble hearing? You're going." Treehorn's behavior surprised Mancuso. His agent never once questioned an assignment or refused to work a case.

"Yes, sir," Treehorn conceded defeat as he terminated the call. His clenched fist failed to crush the phone as an airplane crossed the sky.

Mancuso stared at his phone. Did Treehorn know that the FBI Director had requested daily updates on this case, which Mancuso supplied? Did Treehorn know that the FBI Director, Bureau of Indian Affairs Director, a Federal Judge, and a 'Fourth Man' played racquetball on a weekly basis? Mancuso wasn't stupid. One of the men had an agenda in this investigation. The question would be whether they helped or hindered its progress.

Chapter Three

Navajo Indian Reservation

As the plane transported Treehorn from Albuquerque to Gallup, he looked out the window and admired the majestic desert mesas and stark stone formations. One never forgets the beauty of the largest Indian Reservation in the United States. It covered more area than the state of West Virginia but had only one-tenth the population. Such a contrast it was to the hustle and bustle of his life in Washington DC. At Gallup Municipal Airport, the small, prop plane touched down and taxied to a stop beside what passed for a terminal.

Treehorn stepped down from the plane.

Raven Shelly, a thirty-three-year-old agent who stood six inches shorter and definitely heavier, greeted the new arrival. Officially, Shelly and he were fellow FBI agents, professionals who comported themselves accordingly. Unofficially, once the formal meet was dispensed with, they were old friends. "You can visit without working, you know," Raven joked. He had missed his friend and wasn't ashamed to show it.

Treehorn, less demonstrative. "Washington is only a plane ride away," he parried.

"I'll leave here when the Great Spirit takes me home," Raven stated, "or when I have FBI orders to follow."

"Or when you commit a capital crime and get sent to prison!" Treehorn suggested.

"I'll take the Great Spirit any day," Raven laughed. By then, they had reached the agent's black government issued SUV.

Treehorn removed his jacket and threw it in the backseat and loosened his tie. He hoisted his luggage, one rolling carry-on, and his laptop-cum-briefcase into the back along with the suit.

"Are you staying with your mom?"

"She would beat my head in with her rifle stock if I didn't," Treehorn dryly replied.

Raven laughed, "The only person who can put fear into the great John Treehorn. Drive or ride?" He asked as he held the keys."

"Ride this time, only." Treehorn reacquainted visually to the scenery of rocky buttes and desert vistas dotted with cottonwoods and sagebrush as the miles passed.

Raven's voice interrupted Treehorn's focus from the desert back to the investigation. "I checked with Navajo Nation Police Chief, Samuel Bear. He pulled the Hodges file, not a single update in over a decade."

"I can understand the boy's refusal to report their rape, but how does a man and his vehicle disappear without a trace?" Treehorn focused on the investigation.

"The NNP and our office sent out an APB to every surrounding state the morning the young men were found, and there wasn't a single response." Raven read the file.

"He never left the reservation," Treehorn concluded.

"That narrows our search to only 27,000 square miles." Raven knew the odds of locating a missing person greatly diminished if they weren't found within the first 24 hours. He and his fellow agents worked from two FBI field offices, one in Farmington, the other in Gallup with their administration located in Albuquerque. Raven knew from experience the odds improved in this case on the arrival of his fellow agent to their unassuming sand-colored adobe building.

Treehorn entered the office and Mary Sweetwater, a short stout Navajo woman with a contagious laugh, hugged him like a long-lost relative which he probably was from many generations back. "I missed you!" she said, as her arms held him tight.

Raven stood by and boyishly joked, "Why would you miss him when you have me?"

Treehorn returned Mary's hug, "I've missed you too. How's everyone?"

"Heartbroken since you moved to DC." Honesty was Mary's defining trait.

Treehorn smiled and winked at Raven over Mary's shoulder.

The younger agent rolled his eyes and shook his head.

Mary finally released Treehorn, so the boys could get down to FBI business.

"Where are we set up?"

"The conference room. Coffee's brewing, and I'll bring you some sandwiches."

"Thank you, Mary," Treehorn was grateful for her kindness.

"She never makes me sandwiches!" Raven lamented.

"Let's get to work!" Treehorn ordered as he winked at her.

Mary made a funny face at Raven as she passed him.

The conference room had been prepared for Treehorn's arrival. A Navajo Indian Reservation map dominated the bulletin board. The reservation covered almost a quarter of the state of Arizona, with smaller areas overflowing into New Mexico, Utah, and Colorado. Short stacks of files were ready for his inspection. The speakerphone buzzed and Treehorn pushed the button.

Mary's voice boomed, "Navajo Nation Police here to see you."

"Thanks! Send them in," The agent ordered.

"That was fast," Raven voiced his opinion.

"We knew they'd come as soon as I arrived." Treehorn countered.

The Navajo Nation Police was comprised of 500 police officers, investigators, and civilians working out of six districts. Treehorn and Raven still met residents who preferred to call the Navajo Nation Police by their old name, the 'Tribal Police.' The names may have changed, but they conducted the same business. The agency still worked with, and was independent from, several law enforcement agencies.

Navajo Nation Police Chief Samuel Bear walked in, trailed by NNP Officer Noah Begay. Both men wore the tan Navajo Tribal Police uniform but were otherwise opposites in both appearance and demeanor. Bear, at sixty, had a leathery, friendly face framed by long, black hair streaked with gray held back with a heritage leather band. Noah Begay was thirty-eight and mean-spirited. He entered, scowling, like a perpetual bully. His shoulder-length hair was held together with a beaded band. Treehorn had to surrender his proud heritage when he entered the FBI academy. The two officers nodded to Raven. Their two law enforcement agencies held weekly briefings to address criminal activity on the reservation.

Samuel approached Treehorn and grabbed him in a fatherly embrace, "Don't you have enough crime in Washington DC?"

"Mancuso ordered me here to work on this case," Treehorn provided the reason.

Samuel eyed the young man. He understood the message Treehorn conveyed. He hadn't volunteered for this one.

"We didn't ask for you!" Noah snapped and interrupted their greeting.

"Noah!" Samuel admonished.

Squinting at the NNP officer, Treehorn's hand went to the FBI badge attached to his belt, "This gives me the authority, Noah. I go where I'm told."

Samuel tried to make peace. "He gets his underwear in a twist every time you arrive."

"Why is that?" Raven asked, but Noah ignored him.

"You come when a white boy is assaulted, but where are you when our women are raped?" Noah sneered at Treehorn.

"Hey, this is my jurisdiction you're pissing on," answered Raven as he stepped towards the deputy.

Noah confronted Raven. "You're not doing your job, you little pissant." He pointed his finger at Treehorn, "What are you doing? One in three of our women here have been assaulted. That's twice the national average."

"I start by treating my woman with respect!" Raven shouted in Noah's face.

"Enough!" yelled Samuel before they came to blows.

After a tense few seconds, Treehorn spoke in a conciliatory tone, "I'm here to reopen a cold case, Noah. No crime will go unpunished, regardless of its jurisdiction."

"Funny how time has a way of making you think like that," Noah replied his voice dripped with sarcasm. "What makes this case so special?"

"We have a new lead. Sit down and let's discuss it," Treehorn requested.

Efficient Mary appeared with a tray of sandwiches and coffee as everyone took a seat at the conference table. She accidentally splashed hot coffee on Noah's thigh.

"Great timing, you dumb bitch!" Noah grabbed several napkins to absorb the coffee.

"Oh! I'm so sorry." Mary wasn't apologetic.

Treehorn, Raven, and Samuel remained straight-faced and made no move to assist.

Mary tried to pat the wet spot on Noah's leg with a napkin which infuriated him even more.

"Get away from me!" Noah threw down the wet napkins and stormed out of the office.

Mary cleaned the mess with quick efficient movements.

"You did that on purpose!" Raven voiced an opinion.

Mary didn't respond to Raven. "Enjoy your coffee, gentlemen." She returned to her office with a little skip to her walk.

Samuel responded to the event with, "Remind my balls to stay on her good side."

The men chuckled because they knew Mary.

Samuel's tone changed to serious with Raven, "Watch your back with Noah."

Raven flushed, "He's always resented the FBI." He may not have liked Samuel's cautionary delivery, but he knew to accept the warning.

Raven asked Treehorn, "What's with you and Noah?"

Treehorn and Samuel made eye contact. The Police Chief's slight nod to the agent meant, "You tell him."

"Twenty-five years ago, District Judge J. Wellington sentenced his psychopathic father, Charles Begay, to a prison term of ten years," Treehorn started the facts.

"I understand now." Raven didn't need further details.

Samuel continued, "A week after Begay's release from prison, he disappeared."

"Noah filed a missing person report on his father a short time later," Treehorn remembered the details.

"He never turned up, so we all assumed he met with foul play. He ran with a violent crowd," Samuel continued with his opinion. "I never believed he was rehabilitated."

"His body never turned up. Case went cold," Treehorn listed the reality.

"Noah had to blame someone," Samuel said. "Since no one has reopened his father's cold case, he blamed Treehorn."

"Let's focus on this one," Treehorn ordered.

"I pulled the old file. Where do you want to start, boss?" asked Raven, eager to get started.

"Make sure we have a copy of Hodges' credit card statement and the car rental agreement," Treehorn directed. "Let's attempt to retrace their route. Then we'll question the local boy, Andy Foster. Edward Hemingford is an in-patient at a psychiatric hospital. He identified who assaulted him."

"After all this time?" Samuel questioned, "Who?"

"Shadow Dancer," answered Treehorn.

"A Navajo mythical creature who gathered souls committed this crime?" Samuel scoffed.

"I observed him on the psychiatric ward," Treehorn informed the pair.

"Well, sometimes there's an element of truth, even with the crazies," Samuel admitted with less ridicule.

"I read Edward's psychiatric records. His admissions

have spanned years and his problems all began after the disappearance of Jeff Hodges," Treehorn handed the thick file to Raven.

"Does he remember the crime?" Samuel sought answers too.

"No, he's too delusional, but something has tormented him enough to have attempted suicide multiple times," Treehorn added as he showed them the photos of Edward's chalk drawing of the Shadow Dancer and the gravestone marker image he carved into his body.

As Raven and Samuel examined the images, Raven asked, "Why would he carve a gravestone marker on his chest?"

Samuel followed that with another question, "Did they murder Jeff Hodges and bury his body?"

All three men examined the images. They all knew that Shadow Dancer takes souls and a gravestone marker marks death. Shadow Dancers don't commit crimes, people do. They remembered their childhood bedtime stories. The Shadow Dancer was an old Indian myth of a mother and son who roamed the reservation, searching for the lost souls who wandered endlessly throughout the lands. These souls, either the mother or son, lost their way many moons ago. Sadness will cast a long shadow over them wherever they go until the two are reunited, in death. Then, harmony and peace will follow them to eternity.

Samuel was silent for a moment.

Raven waited for the two seasoned officers to make their next move.

"What's next?" Samuel broke the silence.

"Can you drive me to Andy Foster's for his interview then drop me at my mom's hogan?" Treehorn requested.

"No problem," Samuel gladly responded to his friends need.

"You may take an interest in what he has to say. I want to know if his recollection of events is the same as the boys in DC."

"You think they've changed?"

Treehorn suspected the young man's stories weren't going to match after this many years. Something horrible happened and no one wanted the truth exposed years ago.

Chapter Four

The two of them were soon bouncing along the red dirt road in Samuel's battered police-issued truck into the heart of the Navajo Reservation. A setting sun cast long shadows over the desert, but when the law enforcement officers were on a case, they paid no heed to the clock. They worked on Indian Time. As the vehicle bumped along, the two Navajos silently pondered the investigation.

"Noah was right about the sexual assaults not having been thoroughly investigated," Samuel said.

"I'll recommend an increase in female agents when I return to DC," Treehorn countered. "No woman should be a victim of rape and not have it prosecuted."

"The tribe has failed us," the police chief added, "and the people believe the cycle of violence is a way of life."

"Victims and their families have few options here," Treehorn stated the obvious.

"You did all right," Samuel responded, "and the others, come down to choice."

"I had to leave," the agent voiced sadness for the years he lived away from the land of his birth.

Samuel drove a few more miles before he asked, "Did the boys in DC remember any new details?"

"No, they repeated the police report almost word for word." Treehorn focused on the present.

"They know what happened and they don't want it exposed," Samuel surmised.

"Exactly," Treehorn judged. "Everyone has something to hide."

After a few more silent miles, the car approached a small cluster of adobe buildings and shacks, not even enough to make up a village, just a place where a handful of people lived and conducted business. The gas station didn't post an open/closed option. Everyone knew its owner lived above the business and would pump fuel 24/7 for the natives.

A single adobe dwelling stood out, a small professional structure by itself. The setting sun casts a golden glow on a six-foot high metal and stone Thunderbird gracing the yard. A sign at the roadside announced, 'Foster & Foster, Architects.'

Treehorn and Samuel entered the building that blended with its environment. The agent presented his FBI identification. "Hello, I'm FBI Special Agent John Treehorn and this is Navajo Nation Police Chief Samuel Bear." The pair shook hands with a thirty-year-old Navajo woman.

"Hello, Sage Foster." Her voice was smooth and professional.

"Are these your designs?" Treehorn asked as he examined the miniature house models.

Sage nodded. "Andy and I started this firm after we graduated," she replied. "We've focused on small energy-efficient, off-grid homes here on the reservation. Our motto: 'Good foundations for families.'"

"Commendable." Treehorn's viewed the impressive designs.

"Here's my husband, Agent Treehorn. Would you like something to drink?"

"Water's fine," He replied as Samuel nodded.

"Make yourselves comfortable. I'll be right back," Sage offered.

Treehorn and Samuel turned and watched as a lean, thirty-year-old, brown-haired, brown-eyed man arrived in his wheelchair. The men shook hands as they were introduced.

"Hi. Andy Foster,"

Treehorn presented his identification. "I'm FBI Special Agent John Treehorn and this is Navajo Nation Police Chief Samuel Bear."

"Let's sit by the fire. It takes the chill away," Andy suggested as he wheeled his chair toward the flames. Sage delivered water to each person as the agents chose their seats.

Treehorn, Samuel, and Sage sat in comfortable chairs surrounding the freestanding weathered metal and stone fireplace. The agent observed the sunset as it cast its long, purple shadows across the desert vista and continued into the architecture-designed room. The landscape, bruised by human activity, not only covered the outside, but also contributed to the lines on Andy's face.

"I knew I would hear from someone, someday." The man resigned himself to the fact.

Treehorn understood. "We have new information about Hodges disappearance, so I'm re-interviewing all the parties involved."

Observing the man's gaze towards the exterior, Andy mused, "The desert always gives up its secrets Agent Treehorn, it just takes time." The reflections of the fire and shadows danced across the architect's face and highlighted his pain and suffering.

Treehorn felt the same because he carried the same scars. "Do you wish to talk in private?" Experience told him that men were more verbal when their wives were out of earshot.

Sage spoke first. "My husband and I have no secrets."

Treehorn knew that to be a lie. Everyone kept parts of themselves private. "Do you have questions before we begin?" Treehorn wanted to learn the man's angle in the investigation.

"Did you find Jeff Hodges?" Andy questioned.

"No," Treehorn knew Andy's simple question was essential to the investigation.

"How does someone go missing for fifteen years?" The architect shook his head in disbelief.

"Usually, by foul play. Tell us what you remember," Treehorn glanced at Samuel who readied himself to take notes.

Sage placed an encouraging hand on her husband's arm.

Andy proceeded with the itinerary, "We flew into Phoenix. Mr. Hodges rented an SUV. We played tourist at the Grand Canyon, and then, here on the reservation."

"Continue," encouraged the agent.

"The last night we camped at Sandstone Cliffs in the

back-country near Canyon de Chelly. Jeff said he'd like to have seen Antelope Ravine before we departed. We didn't get there. The four of us awoke the next morning at the 134 and old Route 666 turn-off. We didn't know what had happened to the vehicle. It just disappeared." Andy hesitated a moment perhaps expecting or dreading a question from Treehorn or Samuel.

"Go on," The agent prompted.

Samuel watched and listened. He knew when he needed to ask a question.

"We waved down an Indian woman. She drove us to the Gallup airport. A Tribal Police officer took our report. Peter Garner's plane brought us home." Andy turned his palms upward as if to say that's it. He didn't explain how the boys traveled from the campground to the intersection. It was obvious he and the others were just grateful to be free from an ordeal.

Treehorn's eyes pierced Andy's. An omission is a distant cousin to lying.

Andy fidgeted under the agent's scrutiny.

"Have you had any contact with Pierce or Garner?" asked Treehorn. He didn't specify whether he meant the fathers or their sons.

Andy glanced at his wife who nodded. Taking a deep breath, he replied, "Jack called and told me you had spoken with him."

Treehorn examined the single-page police report. No competent police officer would have filed such a document and Samuel knew this. The agent watched Andy's next response, "I have a copy of the police record. Why don't you tell me what's missing?" Treehorn pressed.

"They dumped us by the highway and Hodges disappeared. Those are the facts-s-s," Andy stuttered.

"What's missing? Did you ask the police officer to falsify this report?" The agent lifted the single page.

"No!" answered a mortified Andy. "I would never ask such a thing."

"Who did?" demanded the Fed.

"I don't know!" shouted Andy.

"Were you raped?" Treehorn threw the verbal punch.

Andy's head reared back as if the agent had struck him. His pale face turned a shade of green. He turned away from the officers to seek comfort in his wife's arms, which she provided.

"Tell them!" she insisted. "They need answers. It's time the whole story saw the light of day."

Andy stared into the fire. No amount of heat from the flames could warm his cold aching soul.

Treehorn listened as Andy's haunted voice described the horrific events that happened to the teenagers and their driver on the reservation fifteen years earlier. "Jeff Hodges drove us to the Chinle General Store. We were all in good spirits. Some Native Americans watched us while we shopped. I remember the contents of the store its shelves stockpiled to capacity with food, clothing, and general hardware articles." Andy stopped to remove a handkerchief from his pocket and wiped sweat from his face.

Sage handed her husband a glass of water.

He took a big gulp and resumed the events, "Ed and I hit the book section. Jeff was busy buying food and drinks. Frank and Jack were flirting with a couple local Indian girls when a policeman approached them. The officer ordered them to leave the teens alone. He said something to them and they hurried out of the store."

Treehorn and Samuel said nothing as Andy took another drink and continued.

"Jeff was acting strange, as if he had seen a ghost. He instructed us to take the supplies to the SUV. Ed and I did that and watched as Jeff used the payphone. When we arrived at the vehicle, Jack was there with liquor and pot he bought from a couple of Indians. They recognized kids with money." Andy gulped more water and wiped his face.

Sage placed her hands on her husband's arm in an offer of continued support.

Treehorn and Samuel pictured the events unfolding as the fire crackled.

Andy continued, "Jeff returned to the SUV, shaken and pale. He drove us to the Sandstone Cliff campsite. We helped him set up camp then we all took turns smoking joints and drinking liquor in the bushes."

The seasoned FBI Agent and the Police Chief watched the tears stream down the man's face as he repeated the night he became a victim.

Treehorn felt the sweat as it soaked his own shirt.

"Tell them the rest." Sage whispered.

Andy held her hands as if they were his lifeline.

Treehorn clenched his chair arms.

Andy resumed his narrative. "The marijuana contained

an added hallucinogen. The cliffs came alive with two dancers, Shadow Dancers, and they danced for us."

Treehorn and Andy's faces paled. Their horrors resurrected. The agent needed to ask but didn't want to hear the answer. "What happened next?"

"Agent Treehorn, we were on the trip of a lifetime then we were assaulted!" Andy's sobs filled the room.

Sage hugged her husband and offered the support he needed to get through the nightmare of being a victim.

Treehorn suffered in silence.

Samuel asked while his friend regained his composure, "What happened to Jeff Hodges?"

Andy struggled to find his voice and when he did it echoed with regret, "We woke up next to the highway. Jeff and the vehicle had disappeared. I'm sorry, but I don't know what happened to him. We all agreed to tell no one, but the doctor knew when he examined us. We told the police officer at the hangar we got drunk and passed out. I had a future scholarship to protect. I wasn't rich like the others. No one wanted to see a police report resurface which detailed drug usage." Andy rubbed his wrists. No one had previously observed the scars on them. "All of our wrists bled from the handcuffs they used to restrain us during the assaults."

Treehorn rubbed his own scarred wrists.

Andy cried out in soul-piercing agony, "I'm in a wheelchair because years later a drunken Indian hit me with his vehicle. I can't have kids, and some mythical creatures named Shadow Dancers visit me in my nightmares!" His sobs reverberated against the adobe walls.

Treehorn stood and handed Sage his FBI card. "I'm sorry. We needed to know the truth."

"Find the persons who did this!" she demanded.

Treehorn exited the room before anyone moved. He strode out of the building around its corner, bent over, and vomited.

Sage watched the agent's hasty departure, "Is he all right?"

Samuel answered as he handed Sage his Navajo Nation Police card. "He's exhausted. We'll need Andy to meet with our sketch artist to describe his attackers."

"Thank you, Chief. We'll help in any way we can," Sage added as she cradled her husband's head in her arms as he sobbed.

As Treehorn leaned against the vehicle, he watched Samuel exit the building.

Samuel went to the backseat where he kept a cooler, pulled out two bottles of cold water, and handed one to Treehorn.

The agent opened the bottle, rinsed his mouth, and spat in the red dirt. He took the remaining water and poured it over his face. No amount of could wash away his pain.

Samuel didn't comment on his friend's state of distress. Instead, he focused on the investigation. "Evil walked among these cliffs and ravines."

Treehorn stared at the moonlit desert, seeing nothing. His sweat-soaked shirt a proven testament that he'd relived his own horror. "I made a mistake taking this case and returning here."

"Do you think it's connected to yours?" Samuel asked as his friend rubbed his scars.

"Let's get out of here!" Treehorn uttered as he climbed into the truck.

Samuel started the vehicle and drove off although no amount of speed or distance would prevent the nightmares now reawakened in Treehorn.

Chapter Five

Navajo Indian Reservation - Antelope Ravine - 15 years earlier

The Shadow Dancer stops his dance and his feathers lower as the echo of the drum dies away. Twenty-year-old John Treehorn struggles against the rope that binds his wrists. Blood drips from his hands, turning the sand red. The Shadow Dancer approaches the woman, who struggles in her attempt to be free. The rope that binds her prevents her escape.

"Skyler!" Treehorn panics as the man touches her.

Skyler Treehorn's legs kick at her attacker, which causes the dirt to form a dust cloud around her. Her legs can't stop the Shadow Dancer as he rips, then strips, the clothing from her body.

"John, help me!" she shouts, as she fights her attacker. Her screams fill the ravine.

"No!" pleads Treehorn. He pulls against the ropes until it seems he will break his arms first before he can break the rope that prevents his release. "I'll do anything you want,

anything!"

*The Shadow Dancer laughs as he beats and sexually
assaults John Treehorn's young wife. The young man watches
as an evil destroys the world as he knows it.*

Treehorn rubbed his scar-covered wrists as he
remembered.

Samuel drove on, the car's headlights illuminating the
red dirt road. He hands tightened on the steering wheel as he
observed his friend touching his wedding ring during the
drive. The agent's long day of police work came to an end as
Samuel entered Anna Treehorn's driveway, but he knew this
case was far from being solved.

His mother's renovated home and original hogan, with
its windows illuminated, was a welcome sight for him. A night
breeze swayed the cottonwoods' branches as if they too
welcomed him home. A full moon illuminated the small barn
and horse paddock.

"I miss her…" Treehorn's pain broke the silence.

"I do, too. She was your wife, but she was my niece,"
Samuel voiced his sorrow. "This case has reopened old
wounds for both of us."

"It feels like yesterday," Treehorn replied, as his memory replayed his own horror film.

"That's what all victims say," Samuel stated as weariness lined his words.

"I work cold cases so that these families can find closure, but will I?" He questioned what seemed as elusive to him as the years passed.

As he stood outside of the vehicle, Samuel's face etched with pain, "I can't answer that, my friend."

The police chief removed Treehorn's luggage from the rear while the younger man greeted the Indian woman exiting the house.

Anna Treehorn was a fifty-five-year-old Navajo woman with all the grace of her heritage. Her long, gray-streaked, black hair hung in a simple braid down her back against her embroidered denim shirt. Her face had just the right amount of wrinkles and crow's feet to suggest wisdom and her posture said she bowed to no man.

"Let me look at you!" she smiled as she grabbed her son by his cheeks. "My baby, you look sad and thin."

Samuel snorted, "City living!"

Anna laughed while Treehorn tried to smile.

"How are you, Sammy?" Anna greeted her lifelong friend with warmth in her voice.

Samuel placed Treehorn's luggage on the ground and kissed Anna on the cheek.

"Good," Samuel hugged her, "family too."

"Would you like to come in for a drink?" Anna offered.

"Thanks, but the wife will shoot me if I get home too late," Samuel replied as he returned to his vehicle and said to Treehorn, "I'll see you tomorrow. Get some sleep."

"Thanks for the ride," The man called after him.

Treehorn and Anna waved as Samuel drove away. Then, she tugged her son's arm and pulled him into the hogan as soon as he grabbed his luggage. Inside the spacious home, Treehorn noticed the new sun room and fireplace addition. "When did you renovate?" Treehorn asked.

"Your father did the work last time he was here," Anna felt blessed.

Treehorn examined the skilled craftsmanship that went into the construction of the fireplace. The mantel held a picture of his father, mother, and himself. A loaded Remington rifle was perched on pegs for display above the pictures. Treehorn rubbed the aged rifle stock. "Nice resting place."

"I thought so too," Anna echoed.

"I love you," Treehorn said, kissing his mother's cheek. The scent of her natural perfume brought comfort to him. "Let me unpack and have a quick shower."

She was both happy and sad to see her son return to his land. Happy to have him home but sad because she knew his nightmares would return.

In his old room, Treehorn dumped his suitcase on the bed. He removed his pistol from its holster and removed its clip. Then he secured them both in his nightstand drawer. He opened his FBI wallet, found his shield and photo, and left his wallet open to the photo of his wife: a beautiful, dark-haired smiling Indian.

He took a long, hot shower in a futile attempt to wash away the memories. When he entered the kitchen in jeans and a white dress shirt, his mother was serving his favorite meal: Beef stew with corn and green chili peppers.

"I made your favorite," she said.

Treehorn's stomach rumbled as Anna served the food. He offered a prayer of thanks and enjoyed his first taste.

"How's the children's center?" Treehorn asked between bites.

Anna grimaced, "There are too many kids and not enough licensed providers. I'd take them all if I could."

"You do the best you can. The center provides a needed stable environment," Treehorn knew this to be true.

"We wouldn't need a center if the parents provided good solid homes," Anna reflected. "There's such craziness now."

Treehorn knew it was learned family behaviors. "The cycle of violence created the instability. Both the perpetrator and victim suffered."

"How can it be stopped?" Anna asked as she cleaned the kitchen.

"I guess family and a willingness to change. When I was younger, I wished I had a brother or sister," Treehorn reflected. "Someone to watch out for me but now I realize I would have worried about them like you did with me."

"As I've told you since you were a kid, the Creator only granted me one," Anna gently replied. Then she prodded, "Now I would be happy at my age to see a grandchild or two."

A painful frown crossed Treehorn's face. "This case has reopened old wounds."

Anna placed a comforting hand on her son's arm. "It's been fifteen years John. It's time you moved on."

Treehorn stared out at the moonlit horse paddock where two pinto horses, a mare and her colt, munched hay.

"Rocky has grown fat," he changed the subject.

"He misses his daily ride with you. I've taken him out this week," Anna patted her son's arm. "He's waited for you."

"I'll take him out in the morning." Treehorn reflected on his love of horses.

"You can help yourself to the flowers near the fence," Anna said as she served her son his favorite dessert of prickly pear cobbler. They finished their meal in a peaceful silence.

As he put his dishes in the sink he couldn't stifle a yawn. "It's been a long day," Treehorn shoulders sagging with exhaustion.

"Good night, John," Anna hugged her son, "I've missed you."

Treehorn wrapped her tight in an embrace. "I've missed you too."

As her son slept, Anna sat in front of the fireplace as the crackling wood burned to coals.

Treehorn approached the paddock at sunrise dressed for comfort in jeans, a cotton shirt, and worn cowboy boots. Rocky, the brown and white pinto sniffed his pockets for the treat. The horse nickered when Treehorn removed a carrot. Rocky crunched his snack while he saddled him and tied his leather satchel to the rear of the saddle. He walked a few steps to where a bed of flowers had sprung up near the rail fence. He reached down, picked a bunch of them, and placed them into an outer pocket of his satchel. Then he swung himself up into the saddle. The leather creaked under Treehorn's weight and its sound that brought alive his memories. The pinto horse pawed the ground, eager to run, and he shot out of the pen as if he had been waiting years for this moment, which he probably had. "Come on, Rocky, let's ride!" Enthusiasm rang in his command. The horse's legs stretched to their limits, its hooves throwing gravel as they pounded the earth. Treehorn rode as if he was born in the saddle, a skill all Indians learned, and never forgotten.

Anna watched as her son departed the yard. Sadness was etched on her face and in her heart. He still hurt after all this time and nothing she could do could change that.

After twenty minutes of natural gallop, Treehorn pulled the horse up and dismounted near a rocky ledge overlooking the reservation. He removed the bouquet from the saddle bag. His grip tightened on them as he climbed a small hill, located a flat stone, and brushed the dirt off the "Skyler Treehorn" chiseled gravestone marker. Treehorn gently laid the flowers next to it, knelt, and offered a prayer.

The sun rose and blessed the day.

Treehorn emerged from his memories after several minutes and the world returned to the present. He observed shifting light on the horizon but heard no sound. He watched as the movement became an object. A tow truck was hauling a dark faded sedan. Its progress was slow and laborious due to the off-road desert conditions. When the vehicle arrived on the dirt road, its diesel engine roared up to normal road speed. Treehorn sprang into action too. He untied Rocky, climbed on top, and galloped the several miles into town. He removed his leather satchel from his saddle as Rocky quenched his thirst from the water barrel in front of the building. He slapped Rocky on his flank sending him home. The horse understood the command and galloped away.

In the Gallup FBI office, Treehorn walked into the conference room. The bulletin board, once lined with a single map, now held several documents. Edward Hemingford's chalkboard drawing of the Shadow Dancer and the gravestone image of his chest carving covered one corner while Jeff Hodges and the four boys' photos were attached to another. "Good morning," Treehorn greeted Raven.

"Good morning. I see you came by Pony Express."

Treehorn chuckled as he removed his report from his leather bag and handed it to his co-worker. "The boys were assaulted. Here's Andy Foster's interview and all of the details. Pull the records of the Chinle General Store payphone. That may take some digging. Hodges made a phone call from there. I want to know who he called," Treehorn pushed a red map pin into the bulletin board.

"I'll get on it," Raven replied as Treehorn examined the map and bulletin board. "Here's the information we have gathered so far. Credit card receipts for gas, supplies, and the car rental agreement." Raven handed his fellow agent the papers except for a photograph which he pinned to the board. The image was the vehicle Jeff Hodges had rented, a white Suburban SUV.

Treehorn examined the travel documents and circled the locations with a black marker: Phoenix, Grand Canyon, Monument Valley, and Canyon de Chelly. The Navajo Indian Reservation perimeter outlined the map. "Their last purchases were at the Chinle General Store. Their back-country campsite was here at the Sandstone Cliffs of Canyon de Chelly," Treehorn inserted two red pins to mark their locations.

Raven examined the papers. "The Tribal Police reported the boys were found at intersections of Route 134 and old Route 666." He pushed a pin to mark its location.

Treehorn's finger traced the map from the cliffs to the intersection pin. "How did the SUV travel across the reservation, in the dark of the night, from the campsite to that location?"

"Indians drive the area," Raven suggested.

"Yes, they do," Treehorn agreed.

"So, where's the vehicle?" Raven wondered if it would be found.

"I know where we can search, but it would be quicker to take your vehicle since I sent mine home!"

Treehorn drove Raven's FBI issued SUV over the dirt

road. An hour later they spotted dots on the horizon, then dots of different colors. The dots, on closer inspection, became acres of abandoned cars. A mute testimony to their past usefulness brought to this desert an oasis of accidents, breakdowns, and abandonment. Every unneeded or unwanted car from one end of the reservation to the other, many with their out-of-state license plates still attached, all found a final resting spot at Nelson Pearson Auto Salvage and Towing. Treehorn drove across the dusty driveway and parked in front of the adobe structure which doubled as the Pearson home. The place smelled of motor oil and hot steel. They entered a room that contained rows of file cabinets and secured key vaults.

Proprietor Violet Pearson yelled into the telephone, "You don't get the car until you pay the tow charge and storage!"

Treehorn and Raven heard the angry response, "It's my car!" then heard the caller slam down their phone.

Violet rolled her eyes and replaced her receiver on its stand. She smiled, and her smile grew upon recognition of her visitors. "John Treehorn! How the hell are you?"

"I'm fine, Violet. How are you?" Treehorn reached out

his hand to shake hers, but Violet swatted it aside and hugged him. She was a tall slim Navajo woman, a couple years younger than Treehorn, and her arms felt as good as did his.

"I'm sorry to hear of Nelson's passing," Treehorn offered his condolences.

"Dad had a good life and I was blessed to have him for a father," Violet reflected. "Hi, Raven. How are you? How's the family?"

"We're all good. I had to bring Treehorn around to show him how to do his job again on the Rez."

Treehorn shook his head in response as Violet chuckled, "I doubt that!"

"How's business?" Treehorn looked around.

"Busy as usual, and you know what they say in the salvage and towing day: 'Pick-Up' is our job..." She stared at Treehorn's badge and stated, "...and the FBI is yours."

"Official business," Treehorn answered for the record.

"Well, how can I help?" Violet offered.

Treehorn handed Violet a photo of the white Chevy Suburban, its registration, and license plate number. "Cold case, in 2001 this SUV with Arizona plates went missing with its driver."

"Did you check with the NNP?" Violet examined the information. "If it's on the Rez, they would have a report."

"Samuel Bear checked, and they don't," Raven stated.

"Violet, what's the procedure when you get a call on an automobile?" Treehorn inquired.

"We transport it here. We charge for the tow, storage, and any repairs the owner approved. Most times the total bill is more than the vehicle's worth."

She removed an old, cracked ledger from an equally old, dusty filing cabinet. "The Tribal Police, at the time, would tell the owner to pay the bill or send us the title so we can recoup the charges."

"This vehicle was a rental," Treehorn stipulated.

"In that case, Tribal would notify the rental company. They have their own contracts with repair shops and arrange pick-up within a couple of days." Violet examined the Chevy Suburban paperwork.

Treehorn helped, "The last known location of the vehicle was at the intersection of Routes 134 and old Route 666 on August 8th, 2001, but it may have been abandoned anywhere on the reservation."

Violet found August 1st in the ledger and searched with

70

her fingertip down each column, looking for the SUV. She turned several faded pages. "My father towed it on May 17th, 2002, from Antelope Ravine."

"Nine months later?" Raven questioned the date.

"Antelope Ravine?" Treehorn questioned its location.

"Vehicles are abandoned all over the Rez. That's why the NNP is notified in case of foul play," Violet explained.

Treehorn looked at the old map of the reservation pinned on the wall and the location of Antelope Ravine. "Does it say who reported it?"

Examining the entry Violet answered, "No. Dad received the pickup call on May 16th. He towed it the next day and filed the report with Tribal Police."

"What happened to the vehicle?" Treehorn asked.

Violet searched the disposition column and replied, "Nothing. It's still here."

"Why would it still be here?" Treehorn questioned.

"Dad had a stroke that summer and I helped out. We must have missed it, but how did the Tribal Police miss it?"

Treehorn and Raven looked to each other and wondered the same thing.

Violet examined the ledger for its location, "Number

902." She unlocked a secured safe. Rows of keys lined the vault, all tagged, and serial numbered. Violet located the Suburban's key, "Here it is!" As she reached for it, Treehorn put his hand on her arm to stop her.

"I'll remove it, Violet." The agent took a pencil, lifted ring #902 off its hook, and placed it inside an evidence bag.

"I'll get my cart and take you to it," Violet suggested since the agents had no clue as to its location.

"Thanks, Violet," Treehorn watched her leave.

When she was out of hearing range, Raven whispered, "How did Tribal Police misplace a vehicle report that had foul play written all over it?"

"Someone buried it for a reason," Treehorn surmised.

"Did Samuel bury the document?" Raven asked. "He's the Chief of Police."

"Why would you think it's him? The NNP has a large staff," Treehorn countered.

Violet arrived in her vintage golf cart, its green and white paint faded long ago by the Arizona sun.

Treehorn retrieved his evidence kit from the FBI vehicle then the men sat on the dusty rear seat. They rode past rows of vehicles of all makes and models, many in junkyard condition.

Violet turned the cart into the row marked #900 and stopped in front of the second vehicle past the sign. Its dirt-covered, faded white Chevy Suburban, its tires flattened and cracked with dry rot. The advertisement decal, dulled by the sun, "Indian Country Tours," still adhered to its rear doors. "Dad always placed the rentals here and if the windows were down he would have rolled them up. Otherwise, he would have left it like he found it." Violet let the agents know the procedure.

Treehorn walked to the front metal tag. "I'll check the VIN number."

"I'll verify the plate," Raven typed the numbers into his phone.

Treehorn compared the number to that on his paperwork, "It's a match to the title."

Raven's phone pinged 'MATCH' and 'STOLEN' appeared on his screen. "It's a match and reported stolen."

The agents examined the vehicle for external damage but found none. They attempted to examine the interior of the vehicle, but years of dirt and grime covered the intact windows, one thing was evident, no Jeff Hodges.

Treehorn shined his flashlight into the driver's side. He found a suspicious item, feathers on the floorboard. "Call the crime unit and have them send a flatbed to take possession," he ordered Raven. He walked from the passenger side of the vehicle to the driver's side and used his flashlight as he examined the floorboard. He then donned latex gloves before he crawled beneath the front of the vehicle and examined its darkened undercarriage with his flashlight.

"We have something." The agent informed his co-worker.

Treehorn stood, removed the key from its evidence bag, and unlocked the driver's door. The door creaked in protest but with a strong tug, opened. Three eagle feathers strung together with a dried piece of leather lay next to the hood release. A testament someone summoned the Great Spirit. The agent took an image of the feathers and placed them inside a labeled evidence bag. He handed the item to Raven, who added it to a larger collection bag.

"Help me raise the hood." Treehorn ordered as he released the latch, exited the vehicle, and the two men raised the hinged hood. The metal screeched as they opened it like an evil spirit's refusal to depart this world. There, wedged inside the engine side compartment and handcuffed to the frame, appeared to be the naked, a sun-dried mummified remains of Jeff Hodges.

Violet choked, "Oh my God!"

Treehorn looked to Raven. "Call CSU back and tell them to send the whole Crime Scene Unit staff! Tell them we have a body."

Chapter Six

Hours later, the FBI Crime Scene Unit staff, dressed in blue coveralls stamped with gold letters FBI CSU, collected the evidence from both inside and outside of the vehicle.

Treehorn and the FBI staff thanked Violet for her kind gesture as she supplied them with food and drinks.

Elizabeth Barney, the senior Crime Scene Investigator handed him a clear plastic labeled evidence bag. It contained an open faded brown leather wallet that held a photograph of Jeff Hodges, his wife Cynthia, and their infant son. On the other side held his prep school identification card. "The victim's wallet was found in a pair of shredded trousers. Money and credit cards enclosed. His driver's license appeared to be missing,"

As Treehorn examined the faded photo she raised a second bag that contained a LEO's standard equipment, "Police-issued handcuffs," she informed the agent.

Treehorn examined them and their engraving: 'Navajo Tribal Police - 1990'. He handed the items back to Ms. Barney, "Secure the vehicle until it arrives at the crime lab. No one is to go near it, and I mean no one!"

CSU Barney nodded and returned to the vehicle to resume her work.

Waiting until the CSU staff was out of earshot Raven asked, "Do you think a cop from the Tribal Police committed these crimes and destroyed the towing report?" He wouldn't let it go.

Treehorn considered his co-worker's theory, "That's definitely a possibility..."

"...or," Raven finished the thought, "someone wants us to believe that."

Treehorn watched as the coroner Dr. Craig Gallagher zippered the black body bag holding the shriveled mummified remains.

"Two crimes!" The doctor informed Treehorn.

The agent's eyebrows shot up, "Two?"

"This one and the criminal that created this monster." Dr. Gallagher's job description had grown.

"One crime at a time, Doc," Treehorn replied to the medical examiner's profiling.

"It's a homicide but I think you already figured that out.

I'll confirm his ID with dental records. COD appears to be a cranial fracture. I'll know more when I examine him," Dr. Gallagher concluded.

The staff loaded evidence bags into boxes labeled "Antelope Ravine - Victim" into their vehicles. Treehorn and Raven watched the tow truck driver winch the SUV onto the truck's flatbed.

The agent called Mancuso to give him a fresh update from an earlier report. "Treehorn here."

"What did you find?" Mancuso knew his agent never telephone unless he found something to report.

"Jeff Hodges' body, pending an official dental records match," Treehorn stated in his no-nonsense way.

"Foul play?" Mancuso clarified but knew his agent never called with good news.

"Appears to be a fractured skull. Gallagher's the M.E.,"

"Were the boys involved?" Mancuso wanted this case closed.

"I think they're victims with knowledge," Treehorn surmised.

"Anything else?" asked Mancuso.

"Shadow Dancers committed these crimes," The agent

knew he wouldn't have to wait long for Mancuso's response.

"Treehorn, your Shadow Dancers are a myth and you said so yourself."

"The evidence points to natives who presented themselves as Shadow Dancers to scare their victims." Treehorn hypothesized this theory when he found the eagle feathers on the floor of the vehicle. They called the Great Spirit. White men don't call an Indian God.

"I want this cleared off my desk. The director received a call from the Congressman." Mancuso was never happy when his boss breathed down his neck.

"Yes, Sir." Treehorn knew when to follow orders.

"Watch your back! This murder was hidden for fifteen years," Mancuso ordered his agent.

"Yes." Treehorn knew that not watching your back came at a price. He paid it once and vowed never again.

"Do whatever it takes to bring the criminals to justice, and I'll deal with the director!" Mancuso concluded before ending the call.

Treehorn knew his co-worker had listened to the one-sided conversation, "Raven, call the Albany office as soon as the ME matches Hodges' dental records. Have them send out an agent to inform Cynthia Hodges her husband's remains were found."

Raven nodded and asked, "Why would someone place a body inside an engine compartment?"

"It's the first time I've seen or heard that, but I think the doctor is right," Treehorn speculated. "There's more to this case than one dead body."

Treehorn and Raven watched as the flatbed truck departed with the SUV headed down the road toward Chinle, shadowed by FBI vehicles.

On the dusty main street, Samuel, Noah Begay, and a few locals watched as the FBI convoy passed. On the back doors of the faded SUV, the label "Indian Country Tours" appeared to wave as it passed.

Samuel watched Noah as he asked, "Know anything about that?"

His fellow officer shook his head, "No, do you?"

Both officers suspected each knew more than the other.

The sun set on the horizon as the officers went home for the night, leaving more questions than answers in their wake, but not Treehorn. He worked alone in his office as he waited for Dr. Gallagher's update. He knew the coroner wouldn't go home until he delivered the definitive cause of death and he wasn't disappointed when the telephone rang, "Treehorn."

"Gallagher." said the doctor of few words.

"What did you find, Doc?"

"Dental records confirm the body is Jeff Hodges. The cause of death was a fractured skull by blunt force trauma," the medical examiner rustled his papers.

"I know you found more," Treehorn said as he remembered the crime scene.

"This man watched his death certificate being signed. He was tortured, several broken bones, and his penis severed," Gallagher added. "It's a vicious attack. You'll get the full report when I'm done."

Treehorn knew from his years as an FBI agent that victims and how their bodies were found provided a vital clue in apprehending their killers. The victim told the story. This one was personal, very personal. Staring out of his office window the agent knew that a great darkness had descended upon this land a long time ago.

82

Treehorn and Anna drank their coffee in front of the fireplace. "Fifteen years is too long not to have answers in a loved one's death. The FBI and the Navajo Nation both failed Cynthia Hodges," he said.

"No one's looked," Anna surmised.

"There's more to this investigation than just assault and murder," Treehorn suspected.

"Yes, and you'll keep searching and find the answers that poor woman deserves," Anna stated. She knew her son would never give up now that he was lead investigator.

Treehorn wondered if Cynthia Hodges would find solace now that the FBI located her murdered husband's body. He suspected she would share his trait, existing as a shell of their former self.

Navajo Indian Reservation - Antelope Ravine - 15 years earlier

Young John Treehorn breaks the rope that binds his blood-covered wrists. He runs to Skyler, his broken and dying wife. He gently folds his arms around her and caresses her face. "Skyler, stay with me!" Treehorn begs, "I'll give my own life to get you out of here."

"It's my time to go," Skyler whispers.

"No!" Treehorn pleads.

"I do not fear death, husband." Her hand caresses his cheek.

"I'll come with you…" His fingers move her bloody strands of hair out of her eyes as she shakes her head. He kisses her softly.

"I'm sorry we didn't have more time," Skyler whispers. "Live, for both of us." Her lips move as she attempts to say something more. She dies with her eyes open.

"No…!" Treehorn yells.

The Shadow Dancer's image reappears on the stone wall. He approaches Treehorn, raises a stone, and brings it down with all of his rage, knocking him to the ground.

Treehorn lands on his back, blood oozing from his head. "I welcome death!" He recognizes the Indian before the darkness claims him.

Treehorn rose long before sunrise. A long, hot shower failed to wash away his memories, only the sweat of his nightmares went down the drain. After coffee, he saddled

Rocky and rode out to Antelope Ravine where the SUV had been found and towed. Petroglyphs covered the outside entrance to the ravine. Two Shadow Dancers were etched on the stone wall. These carved sandstone walls held secrets. The agent surveyed the landscape and wondered why an SUV would be abandoned here.

Noah arrived on his painted pony and interrupted his investigation. "Not your land." His belligerent tone wasn't lost on the Fed.

"This is tribal land," Treehorn said. "Does your family still live over the second ridge?"

"Norma lives at the homestead with her horses," Noah replied. "I prefer to live in town."

"We found Jeff Hodges' vehicle yesterday and it was towed years ago from this location," Treehorn watched Noah's response.

"You were lucky to find it," The deputy face held a deadpan expression.

"This is an isolated area to abandon a vehicle," Treehorn said as his law enforcement training processed the location. "Do you remember who took the information?"

"No report was filed with Tribal Police to my

knowledge," Noah flatly answered.

Treehorn couldn't read Noah. Either he was an exceptional liar or he didn't know about the missing report.

Gunfire shattered the thoughts of the two men. Two bullets struck the ground between the horses, which reared up in fright.

Noah's horse bolted as if shot from a starting gate, while he clutched the saddle horn as if his life depended on it.

Treehorn guided Rocky away from the gunfire to seek shelter against the wall of the ravine. He dismounted and drew his pistol.

Bullets kicked up the dirt behind Noah's horse and frightened the horse to run as if it were the Navajo Desert Derby. The shots were close enough to keep the pony galloping but not near enough to be deadly to either the horse or rider.

The ravine amplified the sounds of the gunfire and Treehorn soon recognized the weapon's distinctive boom. He holstered his and weapon mounted up. Rocky edged along the ravine then dug all four hooves into the embankment and climbed. When the horse reached the top, Treehorn saw Samuel was sitting on a boulder with his Remington rifle aimed at Noah.

Samuel didn't move a hair as he asked with a smile, "How far?"

Treehorn checked the distance Noah had covered as he headed south on his horse and replied, "Far enough."

"Pussy!" Samuel chuckled.

"Try your cell phone next time," Treehorn suggested.

"I don't own one," Samuel replied.

"Noah will never be the same," Treehorn commented.

"He was never right in the first place. I came to find you. Gerald Whitehorse wants to talk to you," Samuel stated as he placed his rifle in its leather scabbard.

Treehorn didn't move. He examined the ravine's location and gazed over miles of desert.

Samuel saw the same scenery, mesas, sagebrush-dotted desert, and a ravine. Not a house in sight on this part of the reservation.

"Why choose this location to abandon a vehicle?" Treehorn wondered if the isolated area held the key.

"We may never know." Samuel's cynicism knew many answers remained buried. It wasn't age. It was wisdom.

"It just takes time for the answers, Samuel." Treehorn

countered.

"Gerald Whitehorse may help you find yours," Samuel offered.

"What does he know?" The agent wondered.

Samuel climbed onto his horse. "He witnessed the attack at the campsite fifteen years ago."

"There's no report of his account," Treehorn countered.

"He recognized the SUV in town yesterday," Samuel added. "He asked me if the crime had been solved."

"Did he mention what crime?" Treehorn questioned.

"He said, 'the night the Shadow Dancers took the boys' souls,'" Samuel's serious spiritual Navajo voice whispered.

Treehorn and Samuel rode their horses around Antelope Ravine to reach Gerald's isolated hogan. The wind howled, and the shadows danced on the red sandstone outcroppings that lined the exterior cliffs of the ravine. Spirits lived here, and their whispered stories blew in the wind. Treehorn and Samuel remained quiet out of respect for their elders as their horses trudged over the water-eroded, sandy ground.

Gerald Whitehorse watched the agents arrive at his

hogan. He was once a tall man, but now stooped in his late seventies, wearing his grayish-white hair in a long wave down his back. He welcomed them into his home. His lined face was friendly as he poured coffee from a pot percolating in the fireplace coals. The hogan was small and cozy, the furniture draped with old Navajo blankets.

Treehorn didn't need to identify himself as an FBI agent. Gerald was a lifelong sheep herder and had been friends with the Treehorn family for decades.

"Chief Bear said you recognized the vehicle. Can you tell us what you remember from that night?" Treehorn asked after they settled inside.

Holding his coffee, Gerald spoke with a slow drawl. "I was on my horse that night searching for two lost sheep. I saw a man with four boys at Sandstone Cliffs campground." Gerald stared at the embers in the fire pit, recalling the events.

Treehorn and Samuel visualized the night.

"The four boys went into the bushes and smoked drugs. They acted stupid." Gerald sipped his coffee. "The man removed a bottle from one boy and threw it into the campfire. The liquor ignited, sending flames high into the night."

Treehorn and Samuel remained silent, respect for the

moment.

Gerald continued, "The man became angry. He searched the boy's pockets, throwing their drugs into the fire." The old man thought of the time long ago. "Two Shadow Dancers arrived on horses. Their shadows appeared on the cliff wall and scared the boys. Two Indians jumped out of the bushes. Their bodies were covered in eagle feathers, their faces painted black. One of them picked up a rock and hit the man on his head. They dragged him to the white vehicle." Great sadness filled the old Navajo's eyes as he sipped his drink. "Scared, the boys tried to run away. The drugs, the liquor, they couldn't escape," Gerald said, haltingly. "They were snared like one-legged cottontails, each caught and dragged into the vehicle." Once again, Gerald paused as he remembered the night. "The Shadow Dancers built a bigger fire and danced around it. They asked the Great Spirit to come to take the boys' souls. A great fog covered the area. The boys screamed in terror as their souls taken." Gerald added kindling to his small fire.

Treehorn and Samuel felt the chill from as if visited by someone from the Spirit Land.

"Was it a man and a woman?" Treehorn asked.

Gerald nodded.

"Did you recognize them?" Treehorn hoped.

Gerald shook his head. "The paint and feathers hid their faces, but they were Diné."

"Navajo," Samuel echoed Treehorn's thoughts.

"Which Shadow Dancer struck the man with a rock?" Treehorn asked.

"The woman," Gerald provided the answer the agent suspected.

They all finished their coffee in silence. "What happened next?" Samuel grilled in his police capacity.

"They released their horses and drove away. I reported it when I came to town," Gerald fulfilled his civic duty.

"Where did you report it?" Treehorn would believe this elder.

"Tribal Police," Gerald provided the truth.

"Who took the report?" Samuel wanted to know who wore a dirty badge in his department.

"Begay," Gerald answered.

"Was it Noah Begay?" Samuel knew the last name Begay on the Rez was as common as Smith off the reservation.

Gerald shook his head. "No, Morris Begay,"

Treehorn and Samuel wouldn't find the answer this day as to why Morris Begay tampered with the police report. He'd died a decade earlier from natural causes. They shook Gerald's old weathered hand and bid him goodbye. "Thank you."

The old Indian nodded.

The bright sunshine caused Treehorn and Samuel to squint as they emerged from the hogan.

"Gerald's lucky. If the Shadow Dancers had seen him, he could have been killed," Samuel spoke his opinion.

"You're probably right," Treehorn nodded.

Samuel glanced at Treehorn. "How did you know to ask if one of the Shadow Dancers was a woman?"

"The coroner said Hodges' penis was severed. I've always found that act very personal which implies a female may have committed the crime," Treehorn provided the logic.

Samuel considered that for a moment. "Why would Hodges be targeted? The five of them were on the reservation for less than forty-eight hours."

"The evidence suggests that this wasn't a random

attack."

"Did someone on the reservation know them?" Samuel wondered.

"The Shadow Dancers took Hodges' life, took the boys' souls, and I think something else," Treehorn theorized.

"So, how do we find these Shadow Dancers?" Samuel knew the agent had a location.

"We start where Andy Foster said Hodges acted as if he had seen a ghost," Treehorn responded.

"Chinle General Store!" Samuel and Treehorn answered simultaneously.

Chapter Seven

Treehorn and Samuel galloped into town. The horses made quick time over the rough terrain. It provided them time to replay Gerald's statements and the investigation. In town, they traded in their horses for an unmarked FBI SUV.

The agent drove Samuel to the Chinle General Store, which was a landmark on the reservation. It was a hub of activity: a store, a post office and a bank. The shelves bent with the weight of food, ammunition, clothes, blankets, shoes, and survival gear. Horse saddles, bridles, and animal-related items covered another corner. A separate area stocked real eagle feathers, beads, paint, and ceremonial objects used by the spiritual keepers of the tribe. Many Indians still considered this section the most sacred in the business.

Proprietor Norma Begay, a short, overweight, fifty-seven-year-old Indian woman, watched as the FBI Agent and Police Chief surveyed the merchandise.

Treehorn always suspected that Norma had a hard life and that no amount of wealth could cure the ugliness in her soul probably caused by Charles, her abusive husband.

"Hello, Norma," Samuel extended a friendly greeting.

"Hello, Sammy and... John Treehorn. Noah said you arrived," Norma couldn't keep the bitterness from her voice.

"I'm working a cold case." Treehorn made it official business knowing that Noah would have already updated her on his activities.

"Who shot at Noah today?" Norma demanded to know. "Did Treehorn tell you about that crime, Sammy?"

Samuel's poker face betrayed nothing at her questions.

Norma didn't wait for a reply, "Is this case one of your own white cases?" Her voice dripped with sarcasm. "We already know you don't solve old Indian crimes."

Ignoring the ethnic and FBI dig, Treehorn removed a picture of Jeff Hodges from his pocket and showed it to Norma. "Do you remember a missing man by the name of Hodges?"

Samuel watched her for a reaction but she turned to her cash register as Treehorn spoke.

"No, why would I?" Norma ignored the photo.

"Do you remember him? You processed his credit card," Treehorn grilled.

For a second, a flash of apprehension appeared on

Norma's face, and then her demeanor changed to anger. "Tourists come and go. It's my job to take their money." She slammed her cash register drawer shut.

"Just take a longer look," Treehorn requested.

Norma glanced at the photograph. "I don't know them… h-h-him," she stuttered.

The agent watched as her face flushed. "Did you know his vehicle was found near your homestead?"

"Just another lost tourist," Norma didn't sound sorry.

Treehorn handed the woman one of his business cards. She didn't take it so he dropped it on the counter. "Call me if you remember anything."

"Sammy you need to find an Indian partner," Norma snapped.

"I already have one," Samuel's quick wit never failed him when needed.

"Find out who shot at my son," Norma demanded.

Samuel sat the box of Remington ammunition on the counter with its cash on top. "I'll get right on that as soon as Noah files a report,"

Norma stuffed the cash into her register, stormed into her office, and slammed the door.

Outside, Treehorn and Samuel sat in the police cruiser.

The agent glanced at the box of rifle shells Samuel purchased, "She remembered,"

Samuel was skeptical. "After this many years?"

"She said 'them' and then 'him'. I only asked about Hodges," the agent clarified.

"Was she involved or did she hear about the crime?" Samuel investigative mind worked.

"Why would she remember more than one person?" Treehorn focused on the finer details.

"The store is a hub of activity for the Rez," Samuel watched as people entered and exited the establishment. "Word gets around."

"Maybe." Treehorn doubted her innocence.

From their SUV, they watched as Norma exited her store and climbed into her Cadillac Escalade. Gravel flew as she peeled out of her parking lot.

"She loves her horses," Samuel said as the tires hit the pavement.

"Yes, she does," Treehorn listened to the V-8 as it roared past them. He then pulled out of the parking lot behind it as she drove past. The agent wanted to see if she reacted if she assumed they were intentionally following her.

Norma floored the gas pedal when she spotted them in her rear-view mirror.

Treehorn's jaw tensed. He drove towards the FBI office but Norma didn't know that.

"She's always believed you were to blame for her husband's disappearance," Samuel remarked.

Treehorn knew the case file. "Charles was a psychopathic rapist and killer. God only knows how many women he victimized."

"He probably got what he deserved," Samuel stated with his law enforcement wisdom.

"Yes, he did," Treehorn stated as a matter-of-fact.

The agent found Raven hard at work on his computer when he arrived. "Pull Norma Begay's history,"

"Norma?" Raven voiced surprise.

"I want to know whether there's any history between her and Jeff Hodges." Treehorn wanted it researched even if it became a dead end.

"I'll see what I can find. I found the records for the payphone after some serious digging. One call stood out near the time frame when Hodges used his credit card." Raven removed the document from his pile.

"Who'd he call?"

"The Baltimore Homicide Division. I called and there wasn't a Jeff Hodges in their system. I left a message with their desk sergeant for a follow-up."

The intercom buzzed. Mary announced, "Andy Foster on line two."

"Thanks, Mary."

Treehorn picked up the telephone receiver, "Agent Treehorn."

"Andy Foster." He sounded nervous.

"What can I do for you?" The agent hoped for more information.

"I spoke with my grandfather's attorney, Robert Kincaid. I told him that the FBI had reopened the case," Andy commented.

"Does he have any information?" The agent inquired.

"My grandfather ordered the lawyer to release all information pertaining to this investigation," Andy replied, "if a case was reopened."

"Was he blackmailed?" The Fed questioned.

"Yes. He said my grandfather received a video and that he refused to submit to their threats. Agent Treehorn, I knew none of this."

"Did your lawyer say if there was any contact with the blackmailer after your grandfather refused?" Treehorn needed the details.

"He said my grandfather received a threatening call. They said, 'You'll pay!' The lawyer is sending you everything by overnight express mail and has my permission to speak to you," Andy stated.

"Tell me about your accident that put you in a wheelchair," Treehorn requested.

"I was out jogging and became a victim of a hit and run. Tribal Police think a drunken Indian by the crime scene photos," Andy concluded.

"Did this occur after the threats?" Treehorn speculated that the accident connected the cases.

Andy paused, "A week later. Do you think someone struck me in retaliation?"

"I don't know." Treehorn didn't, but he also didn't believe in coincidences.

"My grandfather didn't have the money. Do you think the others were blackmailed?" Andy wondered.

"I'll check. Had they ever identified the hit-and-run driver?" Treehorn doubted it.

"No. Tribal Police said there would be no chance without a witness," Andy replied.

"Do you remember the name of the Tribal Policeman who took your complaint?"

"Morris Begay. He was the same officer who took our complaint at the airport," Andy remembered that detail.

"I'll go over the video and documents. Call me if you remember anything more," Treehorn requested as he replaced the receiver. "Andy Foster's family received a blackmail threat."

"I heard." Raven acted nonchalant as he eavesdropped on his co-workers conversation.

His fellow agent didn't mind his behavior. It was easier than having to repeat it.

"I'll call Edward's mother."

She answered on the first ring, "Eliza Hemingford."

"Hello, Mrs. Hemingford, Agent Treehorn here."

"How's the investigation?"

"We've found some disturbing information," The agent sighed, "Someone filmed the assault on the boys that night."

Eliza was horrified, "Oh no!"

Treehorn gave her time to compose herself. "We need your help," He asked in a gentler voice.

"Just tell me how," Eliza offered without a hesitation.

"Can you contact your attorney and give him permission to speak with me? I'll investigate this blackmail." Treehorn wondered what other secrets Eliza's husband kept from her.

"Do you think Edwin received a blackmail threat?" The thought horrified her.

"It's possible," Treehorn theorized.

"I'll call the attorney and have him contact you today." Eliza wanted answers too.

"We also found the body of Jeff Hodges. The boys are lucky to be alive." Treehorn felt she needed to know the latest in the investigation.

"Agent Treehorn, you've seen my son. Do you think he's knows?"

"Yes, I do. Let's hope we can find the truth so that Edward can heal," The agent concluded.

"I hope so. He's been a victim for way too long," Eliza responded.

Soon afterward, Mary delivered several documents to Treehorn, "A fax from attorney Robert Kincaid."

"Thanks, Mary," He examined the papers. "The blackmail request was for $250,000." He informed Raven.

"What's the date?" Raven examined the file.

"September 5th," Treehorn answered.

"And Andy's accident?" Raven asked.

"September 12th, a week later."

"Coincidence?" Raven speculated.

"No such thing," Treehorn replied.

Mary caught the phone on the first ring, "Vincent Pelham on line two."

"Agent John Treehorn."

An older man's voice spoke, "Attorney Vincent Pelham. Eliza Hemingford requested I call."

"We've reopened an investigation into the crime committed against Edward, his classmates, and teacher. Can you tell me whether he or his family ever received any blackmail threats?" Treehorn hoped for some answers.

The attorney paused. "Edwin Hemingford left written instructions and permission to speak if ever I was asked about this investigation. Yes, he received a threat."

"What happened?"

"Nothing," Pelham answered.

Treehorn pinched the bridge of his nose in frustration. "What do you mean nothing?"

"I told him to call the police. He refused."

"What happened?" Treehorn pursed his lips.

"Edwin refused to pay. The blackmailers contacted him a short time after Edward had his first suicide attempt and hospitalization," Pelham described the chain of events.

"And then?" Treehorn's patience thinned.

"Edwin told the caller he would use all of his resources to hunt them down and make them pay for their actions," Pelham added. "My client didn't take kindly to threats."

"Their response?" Treehorn took notes.

"They asked Edwin, 'How does it feel for your son to be a victim?' and that was the last contact Edwin had with them. He was sorry he didn't tell Eliza about their son's assault and he carried that guilt with him to the grave."

"Some victims find it too traumatic having to relive the

memories." The agent knew what it felt like to be a victim.

"Eliza gave me permission. I'll send you the file overnight. Edwin should have notified the police. You can't prosecute a dead man," Pelham added.

"That is true," Pelham's telephone disconnect sounded like the beat of a drum in Treehorn's ear.

Navajo Indian Reservation - Antelope Ravine - 15 years earlier

The sound of Indian drums fills the ravine. Treehorn struggles awake. He realizes that the rope is re-tied around his wrists, tighter than before. The Shadow Dancer appears in his line of sight. "Charles Begay!" Treehorn replies in shock at his jailer.

"John Treehorn, do you know how long this took for me to plan?" he asks with a smile that never reaches his eyes.

Treehorn spits his reply, "I will make you pay for this!"

"Let's see who pays…" Charles replies with a vengeance as he rips Treehorn's shirt off his back.

Treehorn's tanned back shines in the light of the campfire.

Charles Begay, husband of Norma, father to Noah is out for revenge. He raises his prison-tattooed arm; it holds an aged, leather horse whip. Raising the whip, he lashes Treehorn's back, bringing it down with ten years of anger, ten years in a cage like an animal, and for the ten years he was away from his family. "Tell me how sorry you are, John Treehorn, son of the judge who sent me to prison!" Charles screams.

The pain is indescribable as the whip cuts into Treehorn's flesh, but, looking over at his dead wife, the pain in his heart is much worse than the lashes to his back. His last question to himself before losing consciousness is, who is the judge, and who is the jury?

"Two boys were blackmailed," Treehorn glanced at Raven.

"Do you think the two rich lawyer boys have something to hide?" Raven wondered.

"They won't give us anything without a fight," Treehorn knew the law.

"Subpoena time?" Raven asked as he handed Treehorn the document already prepared.

"I know a judge," Treehorn replied with a renewed determination to solve this case.

Treehorn entered an office and closed the door. He filled out a supporting document with all of the pertinent legal and blackmail information. He hit the SEND button on the fax machine then dialed a number he had memorized. A familiar voice answered.

"Judge John Wellington's office," a female professionally greeted.

"Hello Harriet, John Treehorn,"

"Hello John, how are you?" Harriet kindly asked.

"I'm fine. I faxed the judge a subpoena on a cold case I'm working on. Is he available?"

"Let me check," Harriet put him on hold.

Treehorn examined the subpoena while he waited for the judge to answer.

Harriet came back on the line. "I'll connect you now, and it was nice to hear your voice. Don't be a stranger. Will you stop by soon?"

"Thanks, Harriet and yes, I'll try when I return to DC," Treehorn made a mental note to send her a well-deserved thank-you card.

"Hello, John," Judge Wellington's strong and sincere voice greeted him.

"Your, Honor," The agent professionally replied.

"How are you? Harriet handed me your fax,"

"I'm fine. I'm working a murder case on the Rez." He paused as the judge read the subpoena. "The subpoena is for financial records of the two boys assaulted on the reservation. I listed proof for two of the four boys who were blackmailed."

"They're lawyers," Judge Wellington noted. "No lawyer takes kindly to being served."

"They won't surrender information without a fight. Frank Pierce is the son of Donovan Pierce of the Law Firm of Pierce, Long, & Langley. The other is Jack Garner, son of Congressman Peter Garner."

"I see the FBI's requested the financial records of the fathers," the judge examined the information.

"The boys were fifteen at the time of the attack, hence underage. Their fathers and now their grown sons would have paid a lot to keep a blackmail video from the public.

"They never reported the crimes?"

"Correct." Treehorn stipulated.

Both men paused for a long time.

"I..." The judge began.

"This isn't about me," Treehorn interrupted.

"I'm sorry, son." The judge's voice carried a lifetime of regret.

Treehorn believed he understood, "No reason for you to be sorry."

Judge Wellington knew their history would never be changed. "Tell Raven I signed his subpoena,"

"Thank you."

"Will you have dinner with your old man when you finish the case?"

The agent eyed the photograph taken in front of the American flag: Judge John Wellington II being sworn into office by the President of the United States. His disabled wife in a wheelchair held the bible the judge's left hand rested upon while his right hand raised for the oath.

"I'll call you," He voiced with a softer tone. He knew his father's responsibilities in Washington included his family there. He wasn't the only casualty in his father's life. Treehorn was the illegitimate son and it would never be changed in his lifetime.

"Take care, son." the judge said before hanging up the phone.

As Treehorn ended the call, his fax machine printed out the approved subpoena. He located Raven. "Have the forensic accountants put a rush on this and email me the results as soon as you receive them."

Chapter Eight

Treehorn examined the map and the emerging timeline of events. The conference room intercom buzzed, "Yes?"

"Dr. Gallagher on line two," Mary stated.

"Thanks," he pressed the speaker button, "I've got you on speaker, Doc, what did you find?"

"The victim sustained multiple fractures," the medical examiner reported. "I found wood fibers in his rectum. I sent them to our lab. He also had a large quantity of sand forced into his throat and esophagus. I sent that for analysis."

The Navajo Indian agents eyed each other and knew this provided conclusive evidence that Indians committed these crimes.

"Can you send me a signed copy of his death certificate? I need it for his widow," Treehorn requested.

"Yes. CSU has some results that will interest you, but I'll let them tell you." He terminated the call without waiting for Treehorn's response.

The agent dialed CSU and his no-nonsense tech answered, "Elizabeth Barney."

"Treehorn here, what did you find?"

"Gallagher sent me some samples to run," Elizabeth commented.

"Yes, I know," he tried to remain patient.

"The wood fibers are from a Shaggy Bark Juniper common on the reservation."

"Noted,"

"The sand is distinct. Its granulation is from water erosion and the composition common on the reservation in riverbeds."

"What else?" Treehorn memorized the clues.

"The feathers found inside the SUV were a DNA match to a golden eagle colony north of Antelope Ravine," The tech added.

"Go on."

Feeling as if she was on the witness stand, Elizabeth continued, "The vehicle still had a small amount of gasoline residue in the tank. Based on the quantity it wasn't driven until emptied."

Treehorn understood its ramification. "The SUV was driven to that specific location then abandoned?" Treehorn construed.

"Yes, that would be my guess," Elizabeth confirmed. "I found pieces of plastic with a white residue in the trunk area. I'll send you the results when I receive them."

The agent processed this evidence. "Anything else?"

"Last thing, in the victim's wallet, was a business card from the Baltimore Homicide Division, Detective Randy Williams. I sent a photo of it to your phone,"

Treehorn's device pinged a second later, "Thanks, Elizabeth."

"It's my job," she said professionally.

"And you do it well," Treehorn stated in all seriousness because he knew she wouldn't miss a single clue.

The agent examined the bulletin board with the Antelope Ravine area highlighted, pins labeled "SUV" and "Hodges' body" in their respective locations. He checked his phone text and the image of the business card. "Why would he carry a detective's business card in his wallet?" Treehorn asked Raven.

"Baltimore PD didn't have a Jeff Hodges in their system. He could have witnessed a crime or been a party to a criminal investigation," Raven theorized.

Treehorn glanced at his co-worker. "I'll call Baltimore."

He dialed the number and placed it on his speakerphone,

"Baltimore Homicide,"

"Detective Randy Williams?"

A few seconds later, a gruff voice came on the phone, "Williams."

Treehorn reconfirmed, "Detective Randy Williams?"

"The one and only," the cop offered a witty reply.

"FBI Special Agent John Treehorn, Washington Division, I'm investigating the homicide of Jeff Hodges."

Detective Williams questioned, "Who?"

"John Treehorn, FBI. Jeff Hodges, dead guy," The agent could be an ass, too.

"I got that. Who's Jeff Hodges?" Detective Williams tone turned serious.

"He's a homicide victim here in Arizona and he had your card in his wallet," Treehorn replied.

"Hold on," the detective typed the name into his computer. His voice returned a few seconds later, "There's no Jeff Hodges in our system."

"I have observed that people carry police cards if they're related to or are a witness to a crime. Can you search again?" Treehorn ground his molars.

Raven rolled his eyes.

The agents heard the typing. "I have a Jason Hodges… the next of kin, Jeff Hodges his brother." The detective sounded relieved. He didn't want the FBI breathing down his neck or, worse, calling his supervisor.

"Did Jason Hodges commit a crime?" Treehorn wondered how this officer earned and kept his detective badge.

"He was murdered in Baltimore in 2000. Cold case, unsolved. He was a well-known archaeologist. We never established a motive."

"How did he die?" Treehorn's grip tightened on his pen he held.

More clicks on the keyboard then, "COD, a fractured skull by blunt force trauma. The killer tied him to the hood of his own vehicle and beat the guy to death," The detective read the report.

"Are there any other details that stand out?" Treehorn deciphered the clues.

"The coroner reported that sand filled the victim's throat" the officer added. "I'd never heard that one before."

"Did you make a note as to why Jeff Hodges telephoned

you?" Treehorn grilled.

"No, but he left a recorded voice message that's been dictated," the cop added.

"Can you read it?" the agent requested as his fingers whitened around his pen.

Fingers typed on the keyboard and Treehorn listened as the detective read the message, "'Detective Williams? Jeff Hodges here, I met the Indian who killed Jason. You need to call me. I'm in Chinle, Arizona.' That's it."

Treehorn asked, "Did you ever speak to Jeff Hodges?"

"I returned his call the next day, but I couldn't reach him. I left a message with his employer, but I never received a call back."

"He was murdered by then. I'll be in Baltimore tomorrow. Can you box up the file and the evidence for me?" the agent requested.

"I'll have it ready." The detective's attitude improved. He never turned away help in any of his investigations.

"Thanks," Treehorn ended the call.

Raven whistled, "Two brothers murdered: one in Baltimore, one here on the Rez. What's the connection?"

"I'll hunt for it in Baltimore." He turned to Mary and

requested, "Can you get me on a red-eye flight to DC?"

"You're leaving?" Mary wailed.

"No just following a lead. You know I wouldn't leave without saying goodbye."

Raven asked, "What do you think you'll find?"

Treehorn examined the bulletin board and the two sketches of the Shadow Dancers, "The motive for a double murder."

Raven drove Treehorn to the airport for the night flight from Albuquerque to Washington DC. It was long and uneventful, allowing Treehorn to catch up on some much-needed sleep. When he landed, he took a detour to his apartment to shower and change. Then he drove to the Baltimore precinct for his meeting with Detective Randy Williams. Upon arrival, he presented his FBI credentials to the sergeant at check-in. After verifying his identification and his signature in the visitor's log, the officer picked up the phone and announced his arrival. There was a pause then he said, "He'll be right out."

Detective Randy Williams was fifty, bald, and overweight. His gold detective badge peeked out from beneath too many doughnuts. After shaking hands, he led Treehorn into a small conference room where a cardboard evidence box labeled, 'Jason Hodges Homicide Case File #2000-0177' sat on the table. Removing the cover, he extracted a thin folder.

"Jeff Hodges contacted me once a month to receive updates on his brother's murder," he opened Jason Hodges' file. "There were none." An image of an enlarged Maryland's driver's license fell out. From the table, Jeff Hodges stared back at Treehorn.

The agent knew the answer before he asked, "Identical twins?"

"Yes," Williams replied, "but it appeared they weren't close like most twins."

Treehorn opened the file and examined the coroner's report. 'Cause of Death - fractured skull from blunt force trauma.' Additional notes stated that he had a sedative in his system, ketamine, and sand packed into his throat and mouth. He was tortured before someone put him out of his misery. Tied to the hood of his vehicle and sexually assaulted. Date of death, May 16th, 2000. Treehorn removed photos from the box. One showed a man in a bloodied, white dress shirt. He rested chest down on the hood of a vehicle, as sand appeared mixed with his blood poured from the mouth. His pants and underwear were around his ankles, his white buttocks a stark contrast to his bloodied and bruised back. Treehorn removed evidence bags from the cardboard box: a length of rope, sand in a plastic container, numerous documents, and envelopes labeled 'fibers', and various 'lab' samples.

The detective sounded almost apologetic, "No witnesses, no leads, and labeled a cold case from day one."

"Where was the body found?" Treehorn questioned.

"At a deserted gravel yard. Blood found inside the vehicle from the victim's broken nose. His body showed excessive Taser burns. The poor guy couldn't even defend himself. The coroner said the victim would have welcomed death when it arrived. The only DNA found belonged to the victim amazing considering the crime scene."

Treehorn eyebrows rose, "No signs of robbery?"

"His wallet contained his money. The only thing missing was his driver's license. Why would someone take that and nothing else?"

"They wanted a trophy," Treehorn wondered how this man made it to detective grade. He removed the last evidence bag. It contained three eagle feathers tied with a string.

"Where did you find these?"

"In his pocket but no one knows why," Detective Williams replied. "We figured it was work-related."

"Someone called the Great Spirit," Treehorn stated as he returned the evidence bags to the cardboard box.

"I telephoned Jeff Hodges. There was no reply. I then telephoned the wife and she informed me her husband was missing on the Navajo Reservation. I called her weeks later and she informed me her husband didn't return from the trip. never spoke to her after that," Detective Williams explained, "but I sent a report to the Navajo Nation Police for their records."

"Officer Morris Begay?" Treehorn guessed.

Detective Williams glanced at the paperwork, "How'd you know?"

The agent refused to elaborate. "Thanks for having the file ready," Treehorn removed an official FBI file transfer document from his pocket and handed it to Detective Williams.

"You're welcome to it, but I'll be credited if this homicide's solved. Professional courtesy and all."

Treehorn assumed Detective Williams needed to

increase his closure rate. "The evidence from the two homicides tie our cases together. I'll see what I can do," It wasn't the first time someone rode his coattails.

"You should talk to Jason Hodges' girlfriend," Williams added. "She worked in DC at the time as a book editor. Her last contact information's in the file."

"Thanks, I'll do that," Treehorn stated as he handed the detective his business card and the detective handed him the evidence box.

Once outside the Baltimore precinct, Treehorn called Raven. "I'm finished at Baltimore Homicide. Jason and Jeff Hodges were identical twins. Their homicides are connected and both were committed by a Native. We'll have to determine if it was the same killer."

"What's the connection between Baltimore and here?" The younger agent asked.

"We assumed Jeff was the connection. I don't believe that's the case now. Pull what you can on Jason," Treehorn ordered.

Raven agreed, "Will do. The subpoenaed financial records arrived and the accountants have them. So far they've found two payments of $250,000, one each from the Garner and Pierce families,"

"Could be a blackmail payment for the video," Treehorn reasoned. "But I think there's more."

"What else do you want me to work on until you return?" Raven kept busy with the details of the crimes.

"I want you to examine the major crimes database for violent crimes that occurred on May 16th for the last 20 years," Treehorn requested.

"What am I searching for?" asked Raven.

"Jason Hodges was murdered on May 16th and Jeff Hodges' vehicle was called for towing on the same day." Treehorn questioned the coincidences something he never believed in when criminal behaviors were at play.

"That's a popular date," Raven responded.

"Not if you're a victim," Treehorn answered with his engrained cynicism.

Chapter Nine

The Law Firm of Pierce, Long, & Langley - Washington, DC

When Treehorn entered the lobby of the law firm he knew he had the upper hand. No law firm wanted undue media attention if there was a hint of wrongdoing. He telephoned at 8 a.m. and told the employee he would be there at noon. He didn't wait for her to confirm or deny his request, but he thought these lawyers deserved to stew in their dishonesty for a few hours.

The agent arrived five minutes before his appointed time and presented his identification to the frigid staff. "FBI Special Agent John Treehorn." was all he said.

She must have been on the receiving end of a verbal lashing after his earlier call because she made no reply. Her fingers pushed a keypad and she whispered into her microphone headset. "Agent Treehorn's here."

He observed the men in expensive suits as they entered and exited the lobby and wondered if any of them hired this law firm to bury their secrets. He tapped his watch, the one his father gifted him on the day he graduated from the FBI Academy. He tapped it in sync with the second hand. He stood when it hit high noon. He approached the staff and waved his shiny gold FBI badge for her attention.

"Can I help you?" she asked as if she had no clue as to who he was.

"Tell Donovan Pierce he has five minutes before I arrest his son!"

She stiffened at his statement. Her fingers pounded her keyboard, and her voice snapped into her microphone, "Mr. Pierce, the FBI Agent said, 'Tell Donovan Pierce he has five minutes before I arrest his son!', exact words, Sir."

Treehorn nodded once in affirmation and didn't budge from his spot. He watched his watch as she attempted to ignore him.

Four minutes passed then the staff from his previous visit appeared, "Agent Treehorn? Mr. Pierce will see you now."

The agent swore he heard the woman whisper, "Prick!" as he walked away.

The corner of his mouth raised a notch as he followed the administrator down the carpeted hallway. Treehorn once again entered the lawyer's pretentious offices and the door closed behind him as if to say, 'You're in the lion's den now!' He'd been in the lion's den before but, on that day, he was the lion and someone else had the whip. Today, he wielded the truth and carried his FBI badge.

The four privileged white men watched his arrival with an aversion to the law which they swore to uphold. Donovan Pierce and his son Frank held crystal whiskey glasses and, from the flush of their faces, they'd attempted to drown their sorrows for a couple of hours. Meanwhile, Congressman Peter Garner and his son Jack appeared to be stone cold sober. No greeting offered by any of the suits. The arrogant expressions shown from the last visit appeared long gone from the present younger men's personas. All were serious, very serious. Treehorn settled into the same comfortable leather chair they made ready for him. He moved his suit jacket so his gun and badge stayed in their line of sight.

The men unwillingly took their seats.

Pierce began, "We already told you..."

Treehorn raised his hand and stopped him mid-sentence, then used his finger to make a point. "Last time, I got the sanitized copy of the doctor's report," the agent scoffed, "dehydration? That's the story you're sticking to?" The sarcasm wasn't missed on the men.

The four lawyers couldn't stare down the man with the golden badge.

"Agent Treehorn..."

The agent raised his hand and again Pierce stopped mid-sentence. "Let's get down to business. I know about the drugs and..." Treehorn waited for their eye contact, "...the sexual assaults." He added and watched as it ripped their emotional wounds wide open.

Frank and Jack's avoided eye contact read: 'VICTIMS'.

"Why don't you tell me another story?" the agent demanded of the younger men.

Pierce blustered, "I dislike your tone, Agent Treehorn!"

"You have two options," the FBI Agent ordered. "I'll handcuff your sons and drag their sorry asses outside to talk to reporters or you can tell me right now what happened that night." He refused to play good cop today and he had it with their cover-up.

The lawyers contemplated their choices. They could lie again to the FBI and face the consequences or they could tell the truth. The lawyer in each of them didn't believe he knew the whole truth but their time to gamble decreased with each hour this agent led the investigation. He'd found what no law enforcement man before him accomplished.

Pierce was the first to relent. "Our sons were drugged. Are you happy Agent Treehorn?"

He thought what agent of the law would be satisfied with half-truths? The Fed kept his eye on the victims.

Pierce added, "We have a blackmail video."

Frank and Jack's skin color turned a greenish tinge and it appeared they were about to be ill.

"I have a copy, too!" Treehorn parried.

Once again, they contemplated their diminished options. Lying again could endanger the law licenses that they held dearly, but the disclosure of the whole truth would cost them so much more.

Pierce walked to his liquor cabinet and poured himself another shot of Dutch courage, an expensive brand he wasted by downing in one swallow. "Our sons were drugged and assaulted. Are you happy now?"

Treehorn's cell phone pinged and prevented his response. "Excuse me."

A text message from Raven: 'Accountants FOUND $$ -

larger amounts.'

The agent removed a legal document from his pocket and tossed it onto the lacquered mahogany coffee table.

Four sets of eyes watched it land and read the word WARRANT. No lawyer touched it. "I've subpoenaed your financial records!" Treehorn declared.

Pierce went into defensive mode and sputtered, "You had no just cause!"

"You're attorneys. You know a blackmail video justified the search." The agent wanted the truth, the whole truth.

Frank became agitated. "Tell him," he pleaded.

"Be quiet!" Pierce ordered his son.

"He knows," Jack stated as his eyes met Agent Treehorn's.

Congressman Garner placed his hand on Jack's shoulder in a show of support. "Shut up, Pierce!" he commanded. "Let the boys speak. It's time."

The room remained tense but the atmosphere had changed. Treehorn waited and knew there would be no more grandstanding as he watched Pierce sulk and be the lone holdout. The others' slumped shoulders signaled they were ready to surrender the truth.

Treehorn removed a tape recorder from his pocket and pressed the record button. No one objected. "Let's start at the Chinle General Store."

Jack took a deep shaky breath. "We all went inside. Frank and I flirted with a couple of girls from the reservation when a cop told us to leave them alone. He said he wouldn't allow white boys to assault women on his land."

"He'd intimidated us so we walked away," Frank added.

"Two Indians approached and asked if we wanted to buy some pot and booze. They recognized we carried money," Jack stated.

Frank added, "We paid and waited for Hodges and the others to return."

"We watched as the same cop followed Jeff out of the store," Jack continued.

Treehorn removed his phone from his pocket and accessed police photos. He swiped the screen several times then showed Frank and Jack the picture of Police Chief Samuel Bear.

"Is this the police officer who followed Hodges?"

Both men shook their heads, "No, that's not him."

Treehorn advanced his screen twice and held the photo

of the deceased police officer Morris Begay.

Frank and Jack examined the phone, "That wasn't the policeman in the store but he's the one who took our report at the airplane hangar," Jack confirmed.

Treehorn swiped his screen to another police officer.

The two young men nodded, "Yes, that's him." They identified Navajo Nation Policeman Noah Begay.

Jack continued, "He stood behind Mr. Hodges while he used the payphone."

"Jeff appeared agitated after the call," Frank added.

"We piled into the van and drove to the campsite," The two younger men sat back and glanced at each other, resigned.

"What happened next?" Treehorn refused to give them a break in the interrogation.

"The four of us took turns entering the bushes to smoke pot and drink."

"Did Hodges notice your extracurricular activities?" the agent grilled.

Frank and Jack shifted in their chairs but Jack volunteered, "It didn't take us long to realize something was wrong. The Indian's marijuana contained a hallucinogen."

"Mr. Hodges searched our pockets, found the pot and

threw it into the campfire," Jack said as he relived that night.

"The Shadow Dancers images appeared on the cliff walls as the drug's potency took effect. It created an illusion that made them appear gigantic and menacing. That changed when they then jumped out of the bushes all covered in feathers with their faces painted black," Frank detailed the horror.

"The Shadow Dancers weren't myths, but Indians. One of them picked up a rock and struck Mr. Hodges on the side of the head. They dragged him to the car and handcuffed him to the front seat support." Jack provided specific details of the night as if he was a prosecutor in a court of law.

"We all panicked. We tried to run but the drugs made it impossible to put one foot in front of the other," Frank stated the inevitable.

Treehorn watched as the two younger men started to cry as they told their nightmare. Their fathers' faces showed the distress of the burden they had carried for far too long. Frank, overcome by the memory, grabbed the wastebasket and vomited.

Jack found the strength to continue, "They dragged each of us, one by one, into the SUV where they handcuffed our wrists to the inside door handles. We begged them to stop. We told them our parents were rich and they'd pay for our release."

Jack removed a crisp white handkerchief from his breast pocket and wiped his tears. He continued but his eyes weren't focused on the present. "The two Indians added wood to the fire to build up its flames. They danced and chanted in their native tongue. A mystic fog covered the area as the woman whispered in my ear, 'I'm taking your souls.' It's the only words spoken to us in English, the remaining time they spoke Indian."

Frank continued to vomit his memories into the wastebasket.

Jack continued with the specifics. "They assaulted Mr. Hodges first. They wanted us to watch. Ed was losing it more than anyone since Jeff was in front of him, moaning, and bleeding from his head injury. We watched as one of them injected Ed with a drug to subdue him."

Frank said in a flat tone, "He was the lucky one. They thought he was crazy so they didn't touch him."

"They covered our heads with black hoods. The hallucinogens amplified every sound. We felt like wild animals bound by chains. The handcuffs cut our wrists as we struggled to be freed."

Jack rubbed his scarred wrists at the memory.

"It was supposed to be an innocent camping trip…"
Frank's voice came from afar as he wiped tears from his
reddened face.

The Congressman handed Jack a fresh handkerchief as
he focused to continue, "The Indians held us down one at a
time and molested us. Then, the woman raped us and the man
sodomized us. Andy was right when he said we were taken on
the ride of a lifetime."

Treehorn understood their horror. "Go on."

Jack inhaled a deep breath and continued to narrate the
events. "One would drive while the other abused us. Then
they'd change positions and continued their sick crimes. This
went on for hours." Pierce handed the young men fresh hand
towels and waters. Jack stared at the liquor but took a sip of
water. No amount of either could wash away their self-
revulsion. "Every time we attempted to fight, they injected us
with a low dosage of a sedative. Not enough to lose
consciousness, just enough so we wouldn't struggle. Before
morning, they injected us with a larger dosage which caused
us to pass out. When we awoke and removed our hoods, we

found ourselves naked and dumped like trash near a highway. They left our clothes scattered over the area, but Edward had remained clothed."

Frank came out of his stupor. "We dressed and attended to Edward's bloodied wrists. We decided not to discuss the incident. Ed's psychosis prevented him from speaking any rational thought, while Andy's shock kept him quiet."

"What happened to Jeff Hodges?" Treehorn questioned.

"There was no sign of him or the vehicle. Just tire tracks heading back into the desert."

Frank added, "We helped our friends to the highway where we flagged down a driver."

Jack continued, "A nice Indian woman stopped and transported us to the airport hangar. The old Tribal Police officer took our statement, the one we agreed upon. We gave him a story about purchasing the liquor and that Mr. Hodges drove off without us. He called us lucky. My father's plane brought us home."

Sweat drenched the young men's shirts. They'd traveled through the emotional wringer of truth and both had aged years as they relived their victimization.

Treehorn gave them some time to compose themselves but not too much. He wanted to keep them focused on facts and not evasion. No one offered further information so the agent interrogated, "Tell me about the blackmail."

Pierce spoke up, "I think you already know the details."

"Yes, I do, but I want to hear it," Treehorn demanded.

Congressman Garner stated, "They contacted us a few weeks later. They said they had a video and wanted $250,000 from each family. We viewed the tape and paid the money. There was no further blackmail."

"Do you still have the video?" The Fed asked.

The older men nodded.

"I'll need it for evidence," Treehorn stated.

Pierce added, "Yes, but I'm sure it's the same copy you have from the others."

The agent's phone pinged. "Excuse me." He read the message from Elizabeth Barney, CSU. 'Plastic residue analyzed - used in cryo-preservation.' Treehorn's investigative mind recalled the fog. 'They took their souls.' Treehorn glanced at Raven's text, '...$$ - larger amounts.' Money was the root of all evil or was it? Treehorn thought as he turned his attention to Pierce.

"The forensic accountants examined your financial records." Treehorn eyed the attorney. "What will they find?"

"No other crimes were committed," Pierce insisted.

"What's the other payout?" The badge cross-examined them.

"You don't understand!" Frank blurted out.

"Shut up!" Pierce snapped. "Agent Treehorn, no crimes were committed."

A lawyer's forked tongue. The agent knew it lacked the truth and he drove the statute home, "Obstruction in a criminal investigation is a crime. You're lawyers. You know the penalty."

Congressman Garner cut in, "Tell him, Donovan, or I will!"

Pierce's red face illustrated his stubbornness.

The Congressman faced Treehorn and in a calm voice answered, "It wasn't blackmail, per se."

The agent watched as Frank and Jack buried their faces in their hands. Pierce turned from the group in disgust and returned to the liquor cabinet.

"The payouts covered child support," Garner continued. "We couldn't believe such a thing occurred, Agent Treehorn.

The Indians stole our son's semen and used it to impregnate Indian women for money."

Pierce found his voice and yelled as he poured a drink for himself, "They threatened to go public with pictures of the half-breed kids. It would have destroyed our lives, ruined our reputations. Over the years, we have paid millions for child support and their silence."

Treehorn corrected him, "You paid for their souls."

"We paid dearly," Pierce muttered.

Treehorn interrogated, "How many children?"

Pierce hesitated then answered, "Three half-breeds."

Treehorn's jaw clenched. "Don't use that term again. Tell me how it transpired."

"A woman contacted us on May 16th, the year after the boys returned home," Pierce began.

Frank and Jack sat silent and drained their eyes haunted by the events.

Pierce continued, "She informed me of a boy's birth and demanded a one-time payment for child support."

"How was paternity verified?" Treehorn questioned.

"They sent a blood sample for DNA. The boy was Frank's," Pierce answered.

"How much did you pay?" Treehorn asked.

"One million dollars," Pierce sounded proud to admit he afforded such a demand.

"Then what happened?" Treehorn's investigative mind categorized the facts.

Pierce continued, "The same woman contacted me on the next May 16th and informed me of a girl's birth."

Now it was Congressman Garner's turn. "She proved to be Jacks'."

Treehorn verified, "The payment amount?"

"The same, one million dollars," Garner supplied.

"We dreaded May 16th each year," Pierce offered his sarcastic opinion.

"We thought our nightmare was over. Three years, no contact."

"It wasn't?" The men shook their heads which forced Treehorn to ask, "What happened?"

"On the next May 16th, we received notification of another boy's birth," Pierce said. "He was Frank's. Years passed and no further demand for child support."

"We thought our lives had returned to normal," Congressman Garner stated.

"They weren't," Pierce said. "Five years ago, on May 16th, we received notification of the birth of twins."

Treehorn raised his hand and stopped him, "You said three children?"

"Yes, but the twin's DNA didn't match our sons," Pierce answered.

The Indians either assaulted Edward Hemingford, psychiatric patient, or Andy Foster, paraplegic. "Who's the father?" the agent asked.

Pierce hesitated. "You must understand…"

Jack interrupted Pierce and provided a crucial clue to their selfish behavior, "We're the only ones that knew about Arizona."

Treehorn demanded, "Who's the father?"

"Andy Foster," Pierce answered.

"Why didn't you inform him he fathered twins?" The agent's disgust for these four men grew exponentially with every passing minute of his interrogation.

"We informed his grandfather," Congressman Garner interjected.

"He refused to pay the child support." Pierce supplied the remaining information.

"We suspected that but we still wanted to tell Andy," Frank said. "He deserved to know he was a father."

"The hit-and-run prevented us from informing him," Jack added.

"Do you think the cause of Andy's accident related to the refusal to pay child support?" Treehorn let that sink in.

Frank and Jack horrified facial expressions showed they'd never considered that possibility.

"Did the police find who hit Andy?" Jack wondered.

"No," Treehorn replied. "The police assumed it was a DUI, so there was no further investigation."

Pierce provided a clue. "The money delivery should identify them."

"How was the transaction conducted?" Treehorn needed the specifics.

"We sent the money to a mailbox on the reservation at the Chinle General Store. No name, just a number," Pierce added.

"What was it?" Treehorn asked.

"Box 1231."

"Was there any further contact?" Treehorn questioned.

Pierce opened a file cabinet and handed Treehorn two

photo albums, one labeled 'Frank', the other 'Jack'.

"We've received pictures every May 16th," Garner sighed.

Treehorn flipped the pages of the photo album of children's photos from birth to young teenagers. Three children born of two worlds just like him. Treehorn slammed the books shut.

"How did you verify the twins were Andy's without his DNA?" Treehorn asked.

Pierce answered, "The doctor collected samples when he conducted a physical examination of the boys on the plane."

"What other evidence did he collect?" Treehorn grilled.

Pierce stood and walked to a bookcase and activated a hidden button which opened a secret door. He reached in and removed a large wheeled, secured box about the size of a safe. "Here's everything the doctor gathered: we kept it all: clothing, sneakers, fibers, swabs, and blood tests. A lab analyzed everything and the reports are enclosed." The lawyer delivered it to the agent.

"Will it tell me who committed these crimes?" asked Treehorn, angered by these white men's arrogance.

Pierce detailed the results, "Yes, as DNA. I know you'll

re-analyze everything. It identifies seven individuals, Jeff Hodges, and the four boys."

"And the other two?" Treehorn knew who would be identified.

"The two Shadow Dancers, the two perpetrators who committed the crimes." Pierce answered.

Agent Treehorn knew by their attitude that the lawyers thought they had done something right. They delivered the criminals, but there with a catch. "You do know that this evidence may be inadmissible in a court of law since it's been compromised in your hands?"

None of the men apologized. They were out to save their own hides.

"Agent Treehorn, Edward Hemingford wasn't assaulted," Jack offered an atonement.

Treehorn sneered at Jack, "I'll make sure I inform him between his suicide attempts. He's tried several times since that night. Are you aware your silence created consequences? How you could have helped him?"

Frank mumbled, "We're sorry."

Treehorn doubted that but he snapped with contempt at the four men. "I should arrest your sorry asses for obstruction but that's not my call to make. A judge will determine that soon enough. As for your law licenses, none of you deserve to work in the profession."

None of the men challenged the statement.

"Tell me one thing," Treehorn waited until the younger men's eyes focused on him, "Did you ever think of Jeff Hodges?"

Jack offered a sad excuse. "We figured we'd deal with the situation when he returned."

"Dead men don't return!" Treehorn jeered.

"Oh my God!" Frank exclaimed.

"Where did you find him?" Jack shocked at hearing of the man's death.

"I found him under the hood of the SUV he rented for the tour. His sun-dried, mummified body had been there for fifteen years." Treehorn wanted them to never forget their lack of action. Seeing their expressions made him believe he'd achieved that.

Garner sounded contrite. "We have no excuses Agent Treehorn other than we're ashamed, and we refused to put our sons through a trial. No boy should be raped."

"Congressman, no person should be raped or murdered."

Treehorn stood and took possession of the box of evidence.

Frank stood and manned up. "We're sorry, Agent Treehorn. We were young and victims."

Treehorn knew how that felt. He asked the two young men one final question. "Can you meet with a sketch artist to draw the Shadow Dancers? The prosecutor will need it if we can't match the DNA."

The two young men nodded in agreement.

Pierce the blustering lawyer returned. "You can't expec our sons to remember details like that after fifteen years!"

Treehorn eyed the grown men and answered with knowledge and conviction, "They've never forgotten."

Navajo Indian Reservation - Antelope Ravine -15 years earli

Blood and bits of torn skin and muscle cover Treehorn' back from the whipping. He fights to stay conscious, but the pain is indescribable.

Charles yanks his pants down. The Shadow Dancer image on the sandstone wall covers Treehorn's shadow existence on the ground. "Let me show you what they do to you in prison." Charles assault is swift and brutal.

Treehorn focuses on his wife's inert body. He wishes for darkness but for once it doesn't come. Through his gritted teeth he spits, "I'm going to kill you!"

"How's it feel, half-breed? I saw the judge, your whore of a mother, and you the day of my sentencing in Albuquerque. He took ten years of my life. I put two and two together... you and your blue-eyed father."

Charles dresses and adds wood to the fire.

"The jury found you guilty," Treehorn shouts through the pain. His beloved is dead.

"You gave me the one thing I needed to survive in prison: Revenge."

Treehorn recognizes the beat of the drum as Charles drops three tied feathers on top of his face. As he loses consciousness, final thoughts register: The Great Spirit will soon appear and claim him, and he won't be able to kill his wife's murderer.

As FBI Agent John Treehorn exited the law firm he whispered to himself, "I've never forgotten."

Chapter Ten

Treehorn stashed the wheeled case in the trunk of his car with the Baltimore homicide contents and delivered them to the FBI Crime Lab. He knew his co-workers would examine every bit of evidence they contained but before he transferred them over, he copied the DNA results from the Jeff Hodges case file. He drove the parkway to his next destination which was Delictum Press, a specialty book publisher just outside of Washington in Silver Spring, Maryland. Treehorn scheduled this impromptu meeting with Jason's editor, who had agreed to accommodate him in her schedule. He could understand the blackmail and child support monies but hoped she could help him define the motive for the murders. This woman appeared to be Jason Hodges' sole contact.

Treehorn entered the single-story brick building and, once he showed his credentials to the receptionist, he was escorted to the publisher's office. Gina Griffith, a statuesque brunette in her late forties, stood stationary behind her desk and waited for the agent's approach, then shook his hand.

She glanced at the identification he presented. "Have a

seat. I was surprised to hear from an FBI agent."

Treehorn didn't waste his time or hers. "Thanks for seeing me on such short notice. I'm investigating a cold case, the murder of Jeff Hodges that occurred in Arizona. My team is trying to establish whether there's a connection between his death and that of his twin, Jason who was murdered. Detective Randy Williams of Baltimore Homicide informed me you knew Jason prior to his death." Treehorn wanted a verified timeline.

"It's been fifteen years. I don't know if I can be of any help," Gina added. "We published his book,"

"Did you know Jason had a twin?"

"I was told that by the Baltimore detective who telephoned," Gina answered.

Treehorn watched as she rose and searched her extensive book collection that mimicked a protective wall. "Tell me about Jason,"

Gina's back stiffened and the agent watched as her grip tightened on the edge of the furniture until her knuckles turned white. "He was a dedicated archaeologist focused on his work. We contracted his third book," Gina said as she removed it from the wall-to-wall bookcase. She handed Treehorn a picture book titled, 'Petrography of Antelope Ravine'. The cover showed ancient cave drawings with two Shadow Dancers dancing around a campfire. "You can have that. We had it on the market six months after he returned from Arizona. He'd ramble on about that location and its drawings for hours," Gina elaborated.

"Did you have a personal relationship?" Treehorn watched as the color leached from her face. He reached behind him and closed her office door.

Gina stumbled into her chair her composure rattled. "Yes, but I had moved out a short time before his murder." Her hands shook as she reached for the bottle of water on her desk and took a long swallow as if she tried to wash away something that appeared distasteful.

"Please, tell me what happened," The agent requested.

Gina stared off into the distance.

Treehorn wondered if she cared if law enforcement apprehended Jason Hodges' killer.

Her pain-filled voice narrated her nightmare. "We published his book then he started to receive late-night telephone calls."

"Who was it?"

"Some crazy Indian he said he met on the reservation," Gina whispered.

"Go on," The agent knew this victim would tell her story.

"In public, he was this great Native American mytholog expert and archaeologist," She echoed.

"In private?" Treehorn quizzed.

The woman didn't hesitate, "A monster. He seemed to take a perverse pleasure with the calls."

"What happened?" he gently prodded.

She sighed, "I made the mistake once when I answered the phone when she called."

"She?" The agent's investigative mind filed the fact tha a perpetrator and a victim communicated.

Gina nodded.

"What did she say?"

The woman burst into tears as she reached for the tissue on her desk.

Treehorn's suspicion proved correct. Jason Hodges had traumatized this woman.

"She said Jason had raped her at Antelope Ravine," Gir sobbed into several tissues.

"Did she tell you her name?" Treehorn asked for the record but he knew the answer.

"I confronted Jason when he arrived home, biggest mistake of my life."

"I'm sorry." The agent offered his sympathy.

"He was one sick bastard!" Gina echoed the pain she suffered, "I ran and I never looked back." Pointing to the book that Treehorn held, "He dedicated it to the woman he assaulted then sent her a copy with his telephone number. Can you believe he would do that?"

The agent turned the dedication page and read: 'To the Shadow Dancers, Norma Begay and her son. Thanks for the dance at Antelope Ravine.'

"No one's crying over his death only how he lived his life," She buried her face in her hands and sobbed.

"I'm sorry. I had to know." He left his business card on the corner of her desk and departed the building.

Treehorn had seen it in crime after crime where a victim was in the wrong place at the wrong time. Jason Hodges had committed the original sin at Antelope Ravine. Jeff, the innocent twin, set in motion his own fate. He'd come to the reservation as a tourist, met, then died at the hands of the victim his brother had raped. The motive may bring a murderer to justice but the question remained, who actually killed Jeff and Jason Hodges?

The Fed arrived at his FBI office to find that the agents and staff had long departed for the night. The janitors worked his area but soon moved away to give him privacy. He opened his case and removed the DNA results of the tested evidence and telephoned his fellow agent.

Raven picked up the telephone on the first ring. "Agent Shelly."

"Treehorn here." It felt good to hear his friend's voice.

"Did we catch the bad guy?" It was a long-standing conviction between friends.

"Yes and no. Jason Hodges came to the Rez seventeen years ago and he stole two spirits," Treehorn reported. "Did you get any hits from the major crimes database?"

"The hospitals and clinics had nothing, so I contacted the medicine men and women," Raven replied. "Lucy Yazzie remembered treating a victim of a vicious assault, but the woman refused to report it, and Lucy couldn't release the victim's name to me."

Treehorn the female, "She confirmed a woman had been raped at Antelope Ravine on May 16th, 1999 right?"

His friend and LEO voiced his surprise, "Yes. Do you know the victim?"

"We both do. It's Norma Begay," Treehorn sighed.

"Who attacked her?" Raven asked.

"Jason Hodges," His co-worker answered.

"How'd you learn that?" He observed since his own graduation from the FBI Academy his friend Treehorn excelled at two things: his proven investigative skills and his Navajo intuition.

"Jason Hodges' book publisher provided me with proof. It was right in front of us. He came to the reservation and assaulted Norma."

"Did Norma murder Jason Hodges and then his brother?" Raven asked. "I don't see her being capable of that."

Treehorn thought otherwise. "The doctor examined the boys after their assaults and kept a box of evidence which I delivered to the lab for analysis. There were two unidentified DNA samples found. They'll provide the identification and proof of who kidnapped and assaulted the kids. I don't know if

155

it will prove murder."

"Did the men give answers to the blackmail and payouts?"

"Yes, I'll fill you in when I arrive," Treehorn said.

"When are you returning?"

"My flight leaves in a little over two hours. Keep this information quiet."

"Understood. I'll meet you at the airport," Raven offered.

"Thanks." Treehorn ended the call.

Treehorn accessed the US Department of Homeland Security website for the TSA. He clicked on 'Passenger Flight Records' and typed in the information he needed: Albuquerque to Baltimore, Round Trip. Date: May 10th to 20th, 2000. First Name: 'Norma'. Last Name: 'Begay'. He hit 'ENTER'. The computer returned: NO RESULTS. Treehorn deleted 'Norma' and left the 'First Name' space blank and hit 'ENTER'. One name appeared: NOAH BEGAY. He then accessed the secured website 'Native American Indian Tribes clicked on 'DNA Database' then on 'Navajo'. The agent removed the manila folder labeled 'DNA Results' that he copied from Donovan Pierce's evidence box. He turned to the pages that identified Jeff Hodges and the four boys, then stopped at the two labeled 'Unknown Suspect #1' and 'Unknown Suspect #2'. His fingers typed in the computer search form with the information listed from the 'DNA Results' document for the Unknown Suspects #1 and #2. He clicked 'ENTER' and waited for the data results.

He stared at the framed photograph on his desk: two Shadow Dancers, his mother and him. The computer beeped: 'DNA Match'. Treehorn clicked on the icon. The rape, kidnapping, and blackmail suspects officially appeared: Norma and Noah Begay, mother and son, two Shadow Dancers. Noah had to have killed Jason Hodges but he left no DNA evidence. The agent knew the lab would match the eagle feathers he found on Jason's body to the ones found in Jeff's SUV. It was probably the only evidence that tied the two murders together, but it still wasn't a conviction for either murder. He assumed it was either Norma or Noah. He had enough to arrest them now.

Treehorn whispered to himself, "Never leave your DNA at any crime scene when it can be verified by the Navajo

Nation Tribal database." He hit 'SAVE'. Then he clicked on his legal page, chose the 'ARREST WARRANT and SUBPOENA' icon and typed in 'NORMA BEGAY' and 'NOAH BEGAY,' then he hit 'FORWARD' to Raven who would sign it and forward it to 'JUDGE JOHN WELLINGTON II'. Treehorn avoided a conflict of interest. He then emailed Leo Mancuso, 'Identified rapists and kidnappers, Norma and Noah Begay. I'm returning to the reservation to arrest them.' He signed 'Treehorn' and pressed the 'SEND' button. He sent a confidential email to Raven wi the results, "Forward subpoena to Judge W. and have the mer ready." Treehorn shut off his computer and grabbed his suitcase to catch a ride to the airport. Severe thunderstorms delayed his return flight to Albuquerque. He felt that the Creator had intervened and allowed him time to rest.

Raven transported his friend from the airport. "I can't believe Norma and Noah attacked those boys." No amount of years with the FBI could desensitize the two agents when someone they knew had committed a shocking crime.

"We're all capable, Raven, even you," Treehorn emphasized.

158

"I know, but I thank the Great Spirit I've never had to make that choice," Raven echoed.

"Let's hope you never have to." Treehorn understood choices. He's lived with them. Darkness had fallen by the time the agents arrived at their FBI office. Treehorn threw down his suitcase and entered the locker room. He removed his shirt and white t-shirt at his locker. His scar-covered back was similar to those seen on the Negro slaves of the Old South, shiny and laced with thick keloid tissue. He dressed and returned to the main conference room in his black tactical gear, which he covered with his FBI-labeled bulletproof vest. He glanced at the bulletin board that now held the photos of Jason Hodges, Norma, and Noah Begay. Treehorn wondered as a Navajo, an agent, and as a man if the vicious circle of violence would end tonight for these two.

Raven entered dressed in black.

Samuel followed, similarly outfitted with his black ammunition bag.

"Thanks for coming," Treehorn's grim tone voiced the seriousness of the situation.

"It's not an invitation I wanted," Samuel replied. "I can't believe Noah's involved."

"Or Norma," Raven added.

"Anyone is capable," Samuel reiterated. "All it takes is the right circumstances."

Treehorn and Raven looked at each other as Samuel repeated their words.

Raven checked his guns, "I'll ask him when we apprehend him."

Treehorn checked his own weapons, the pistol on belt, and his ankle holster.

Mary entered and delivered the arrest warrants to Raven. "I'm sorry to hear this happened to that little prick,"

Samuel smiled, "Honest to a fault."

Mary returned to her office as five armed agents dressed in similar black FBI tactical gear joined them.

Treehorn conducted the briefing. "Two suspects wanted for felony kidnapping, sexual assault, and blackmail. We have them on suspicion of the murder of two individuals connected to the case."

"He's one of ours so you know the drill," Samuel warned and the others understood the risks.

Raven handed the officers the legal documents. "Here's the arrest warrants for Norma and Noah Begay, with their photos."

The LEOs examined the images, paperwork, and slid them into their Velcro-secured pockets.

Treehorn assigned duties to his fellow officers, "Morales and Mortensen, you take Norma Begay's residence." The two agents checked their weapons. "Johnson and Watson, you'll take Norma Begay's store." The two officers nodded and bumped fists. "Chief Bear, Agents Shelly, Paine, and I will take Noah Begay's residence. Any questions?" No one spoke. They've heard this song and dance before and knew the drill. "Everyone is to maintain radio silence unless it's a dire emergency," Treehorn ordered.

"Noah has access to all police communication equipment," Samuel reiterated. "He'll monitor it and use it against us."

"Consider them both armed and dangerous. Let's roll!"

The men exited the building, placed their weapons and ammunition bags in the rear compartments of the three unmarked black SUVs, and drove away toward their targeted locations.

Chapter Eleven

One SUV headed to Norma Begay's home while the other drove to the Chinle General Store. Treehorn drove to Noah's house. He stopped his vehicle with its lights off on a section of desert road a couple hundred feet from the structure. The house sat in darkness, with no sign of his vehicle in its driveway. The agents approached the dwelling in stealth mode with their pistols in their hands. Treehorn and Samuel took the front entrance while Raven and Agent Paine took the rear. Treehorn tried the doorknob and found it unlocked, a common occurrence on the Rez, so he and Samuel entered. They listened for a presence but all was silent. The two other agents entered from the rear. Samuel turned on the lights.

"Tear it apart!" Treehorn ordered.

The latex-gloved agents went to work and searched the clean single bedroom home. After several minutes into the examination, Raven found a hidden compartment in the bedroom wall behind a Navajo print depicting Antelope Ravine. The secret area held a small unsecured metal box that the agent gently removed and placed on the bed. He opened the lid and examined its contents.

Raven called Treehorn. "We found something!"

Treehorn entered the room as the contents of the box were removed. A passport, pistol, ammunition, sex magazines, financial papers, a DVD, and a driver's license were inside. He handed the license to Treehorn who examined it. "Jason Hodges."

Raven asked Treehorn, "Why would he keep it?"

"A trophy for the murder." Treehorn guessed a second time in this investigation.

The men heard the vehicle approach and failed to shut off the house lights in time.

Treehorn pulled his weapon and ran for the door as he saw the headlights.

Noah recognized the FBI's black SUV and understood the implications as to why the agents searched his house. He floored the gas pedal and sped away as the Fed exited the home, then stood in Noah's dust trail.

The agent shoved his pistol in its leather holster as the vehicle sped away, frustrated at his rookie mistake.

Raven ordered Agent Paine, "Stay here and secure the place for CSU."

Treehorn, Samuel, and Raven jumped inside the SUV. The man floored the gas pedal as soon as Samuel and Raven's doors closed. He followed Noah's red taillights through the back-country dirt roads on the reservation, bouncing over the ruts and sagebrush.

Samuel telephoned the NNP dispatch to ready a helicopter with his deputies. They connected the helicopter's guidance system to FBI's vehicle. "He can only run so far before he's cornered," he added.

"I know where he's going," Treehorn said as he followed Noah over the rugged desert terrain, dry washes, and past rock formations. He kept the SUV back a distance so Noah wouldn't have a reason to shoot at them.

"Where?" Raven asked from the rear seat.

Samuel answered for his friend, "Antelope Ravine."

"Why there?" Raven questioned.

Treehorn drove past the outcropping of red sandstone and its entrance sign. "This is where Norma's life-spirit ended years ago at the hands of Jason Hodges." He knew this was where it had all begun.

Treehorn stopped the SUV a hundred yards from

Antelope Ravine's entrance. The men spotted Noah's vehicle parked next to Norma's white Escalade. They scrambled out and hid behind a sandstone rock outcropping. The light of the full moon illuminated the sheer beauty of the rocks like a silver dream or white nightmare.

"Why's Norma here?" Samuel whispered.

Treehorn speculated, "Noah called her when he found us at his house. One or both of them killed Jeff Hodges and it ends here tonight."

The police chief called his command center on his satellite phone, "Dispatch, this is Police Chief Samuel Bear. Contact Helo 2 and ask them their arrival time at Antelope Ravine."

The men waited to hear Samuel's response from the Navajo Nation Police as gave orders, "Inform them of our location at the south entrance. Come in dark. I don't want our chopper or its officers shot."

"What's their ETA?" Raven watched for any activity.

"They're thirty minutes out," Samuel checked his watch.

"I'm not waiting," Treehorn left the shelter of the rocks and opened the rear set of doors of his SUV. He remained hidden behind them as he accessed the cache of weapons.

166

Samuel unfastened his own bag, which contained his own NNP rifles.

Each man selected their preferred weapon, inserted an ammunition clip, and loaded the first round into its chamber. The agent asked, "Are we ready?" Samuel and Raven nodded.

"He won't surrender," Raven said what was on everyone's mind.

"I know, but we have to try," Treehorn countered.

Samuel added, "We owe him that as a friend and fellow officer."

"Can we hope they'll both surrender?" Raven checked his weapon.

Treehorn and Samuel offered no response. No one wanted to take down someone they knew.

"Ready? I'll search Norma's vehicle, you two have Noah's," Treehorn ordered.

The three men nodded and ran to the vehicles with their weapons drawn.

Samuel and Raven gulped air, half from exertion, the other from adrenaline. They aimed their guns inside but found Noah's empty.

Samuel wheezed, "I need to get to the gym!"

167

"I'll come with you," Raven gasped.

Treehorn joined the men after he searched Norma's Escalade and showed no signs of exertion. "I'll take the east path, you two take the west."

"Keep your head down," Samuel said. "Noah's passed all of his ballistic tests."

Treehorn added, "Bullets don't ricochet off sandstone, but don't think one can't strike us."

Gunshots greeted the agents when they entered the ravine. The agent sought shelter in one direction, Samuel and Raven in another.

Treehorn shouted, "Give it up, Noah, before anyone gets hurt!"

Noah replied, "We all know how this is going to end!"

"Surrender now, Noah!" Samuel ordered.

"We know what happened," Treehorn shouted.

"You don't know everything!" The deputy yelled.

"We know your mother was sexually assaulted by Jason Hodges. That's an extenuating circumstance. A judge would take that into consideration."

"Like the judge who sentenced my old man to ten years

in prison?" Noah reloaded his pistol.

"We can't be blamed for the sins of our fathers," Treehorn replied. "Give up before someone gets shot." He crawled from rock to rock to get closer to Noah.

Samuel and Raven made the same movement from the other direction.

"Is that little pissant, Raven, with you?" Noah demanded.

Samuel raised his hand and motioned Raven to remain quiet.

Noah continued, "Tell him to pop his head up and I'll put a bullet in it."

Samuel placed his fingers on his lips silently telling Raven to not make a sound.

"I know about Baltimore." The agent surrendered that information so Noah focused on him. "I need to take you in."

"You know, she was never the same," Noah countered.

Treehorn understood. Some people never recovered after becoming a victim.

"I know Noah..." The man replied, "...and I understand."

"She's always blamed me. I couldn't understand why she did that," he cried.

"It wasn't your fault Noah," Treehorn empathized.

Noah saw their shadows move in the moonlight. "No, you don't!" He fired at the shadows and an unlucky ricochet struck Raven.

The younger agent fell to the ground as blood covered his arm.

"Raven's hit," Samuel yelled as he grabbed his handkerchief and tied it around the wound to stop the bleeding.

"That burns." Raven whispered, "It's a through and through."

Treehorn was furious at his fellow agent's injury. He knew this was going to turn deadly. "Noah, let's end this now!"

"Does it hurt you, you little pissant?" Noah demanded. "Samuel, I want you to know you were a good boss."

"Don't do anything stupid!" Samuel pleaded.

Noah walked out into the moonlight and pointed his gun at the agents as they sheltered behind large boulders.

"I don't want to shoot you, Noah," Treehorn implored. "Put the weapon down."

Noah said with an edge of resignation, "I don't fear death."

"Neither do I, but now is not our time," The agent cautioned.

Noah continued to cry. "It didn't matter what I did. I committed murder for her, not once, but twice. It was never enough!"

"Put down the gun Noah!" Treehorn ordered.

"I'm not going to prison," Noah said with finality. "I'd never survive."

"Lower your weapon," Treehorn pleaded. "Let's end this." The agent moved out from behind the boulder with his weapon drawn.

Noah lowered his revolver as he gazed down at his Navajo Nation Police badge he mused, "She told me that one day I would die in this uniform. She was right." He raised his gun toward Treehorn.

Gunshots erupted. Bullets peppered Noah's back. Treehorn sought cover as Noah, in shock, looked at his pristine uniform before he fell backward to the ground. Treehorn pointed to the location where the shots originated. Samuel and Raven understood the gesture. They emptied their clips at the only person believed to be in that direction and provided cover for Treehorn as he ran to help Noah. The shooter, who had to be Norma, used the darkness to remain silent out of sight and out of range from Samuel and Raven's bullets.

Samuel reloaded his weapon while Raven struggled to do the same. The chief reached over and removed Raven's ankle-holstered gun and handed it to him. "Stay here…" He ordered his friend, "…and don't get shot again." Samuel fired his gun once into the ravine and entered the darkness to track Norma. A talent he excelled at and his prey knew it.

Raven stood guard in case she doubled back and aimed for his fellow agent.

Treehorn knelt beside the downed officer.

Noah's blood colored the sand redder as he bled out. He hadn't worn his bulletproof vest.

"Noah! Where's your protection?" Treehorn criticized.

"I asked her to meet me here so we could make it right," Noah struggled to breathe.

The injured officer stretched out his hand and Treehorn grasped it. "Tell her I forgive her," he begged.

"I'll find a way," he offered.

Noah whispered his words, "I think she killed my father."

"She didn't," Treehorn confessed. He didn't know if Noah heard him or not as the Great Spirit claimed his soul. He lowered his head in silent prayer. Raven approached quietly in respect.

Samuel returned from his search for Norma.

"Norma?" Treehorn holstered his weapon.

Samuel shook his head. "She disappeared deeper into the ravine."

"How could Norma shoot her own son?" Raven demanded.

No one knew had an answer in the wake of the tragedy.

Treehorn examined Raven's injury, "Let's take care of that."

As the three exited the ravine's entrance, Treehorn removed his pistol and fired a bullet in both of Norma and Noah's front tires. "She's not driving out of here."

They heard the Navajo Nation Police helicopter near. The Police Chief radioed his staff, "Samuel Bear here. I'll light up the landing with a flare." He grabbed one, activated it, and ran a safe distance to a flat area where the chopper could safely land. As soon as the helicopter touched the ground, he snuffed it out returned to the men.

"Samuel, have your helicopter drop you and your men off at the north end of the ravine so Norma can't escape; then, have it transport Raven to the hospital." Treehorn finished bandaging Raven's wound. "You're lucky. It missed the artery."

"Thanks!" Raven winced as he moved his arm. "I guess I'm lucky he missed my head."

"Yes, you are," Treehorn scolded.

"What's Norma waiting for?"

"Me," Treehorn answered, "I'll take this entrance."

The two older men eyed each other. They knew what needed to be done.

"Norma will never leave the reservation," Raven offered his opinion.

"She has two options..." Treehorn said as he reloaded his pistol. "...prison or the Great Spirit."

The agent gripped each of his friend's shoulders. He didn't utter a word to show that he cared.

"Watch your front," Raven stated.

"Watch your back," Samuel said as he nodded toward

the injured FBI agent, "My men will watch the pissant."

"Hey!" Raven protested.

Treehorn shoved two large bandages and a roll of surgical tape into Raven's pocket then handed him water. "That may get you a couple days off after speaking to Mancuso."

Raven frowned, "I'll start the paperwork at the hospital. You be careful." He turned and walked away before his friend could comment.

They all knew the seriousness of the situation.

Samuel and Treehorn looked at each other. The Police Chief knew his friend might not survive, but he knew he had to finish what had begun fifteen years earlier. He leaned in and hugged him like a son, "Today is not your day to die, my friend."

Treehorn returned his hug, "The Great Spirit knows when and where."

"My boys and I'll meet you in the middle. She won't get past us," Samuel turned to board the helicopter.

"Thanks, Samuel." Treehorn aimed his rifle at the ravine's opening as the helicopter took flight, without incident.

Samuel watched as the agent he treated like a son held his rifle and disappeared into sandstone ravine. He knew the man would reach Norma before he and his deputies would.

"He won't let Norma get the jump on him," Raven yelled over the noise.

"He ordered us out of harm's way," Samuel shouted. H wondered if his friend had a plan for removing them. The police chief would bet his badge that if Treehorn had a motiv he'd take it with him to his grave.

Samuel thought about Norma and Treehorn on the fligh to Antelope Ravine's north entrance. Two Shadow Dancers entered the ravine, one mother and one son. He knew by sunrise, one would walk on the reservation, and the other would be with the Great Spirit. As soon as he and his deputie disembarked, the helicopter departed for the hospital.

Raven watched from the air as his fellow armed LEOs disappeared into the ravine's entrance in search of a killer. H offered a prayer for all of their safety.

Meanwhile, at the other end, Treehorn had progressed further into the ravine. He heard a coyote yip-howl in pain as if it knew a terrible darkness had descended over the reservation. The hairs rose on Treehorn's neck. The coyote foretold the story. Someone would die tonight.

Chapter Twelve

Treehorn's chest felt like a beating drum as he crept deeper into Antelope Ravine. It was the first time he had entered the sandstone canyon since Skyler's death.

Navajo Indian Reservation - Antelope Ravine - 15 years earlier

Treehorn's universe has two elements: pain and darkness. The beat of the drum causes him to open his eyes and focus on the Indian petroglyph, the images carved in the stone that depict his mother's heritage. Shadow Dancers are on the wall, Mother and Son. Fighting consciousness, Treehorn mutters, "Mother..."

Charles's voice cuts this thoughts, "Do you fear death, half-breed?"

The Indian sees the white light that calls. He feels peace for his journey.

"No," he surrenders to the Spirits, "Do you?"

Charles watches as his victim succumbs to his chosen

path.

Treehorn concentrated on navigating the ravine's eroded sandy, gravel-filled path. Norma was in here with a loaded gun, and she excelled at its usage with proven deadly force. She had a temporary advantage over the Navajo agent in that she knew Antelope Ravine like the back of her hand, but he had Samuel and his deputies approaching from the north. She wouldn't get past either party. The clouds passed and the moonlight once again highlighted the interior of the canyon. It's natural beauty carved by decades of rains that eroded and created small caverns with sandstone weathered outcroppings. Its darkened crevices could conceal a deadly shooter.
Treehorn's eyes adjusted without using his flashlight, a target Norma could hit at any distance within these walls. He opened his mind through the pain of his last visit here and he realized where he would soon find Noah's killer. The agent proceeded slowly across the sand. He observed the glow of a campfire a few hundred feet ahead as he rounded a sharp curve cut in the sandstone. The flames of the fire illuminated the beauty and tragedy of the red walls. Sporadic flooding left burnable debris throughout the floor of the canyon that provided adequate

tinder for combustion. The smoke and sparks drifted skyward as he approached the glow. He knew Norma waited for him and she didn't disappoint.

The agent entered with his weapon drawn and passed her rifle, which she had perched against a boulder. He found her exactly where expected, sitting in front of the fire with her revolver pointed at him.

"Norma," the agent acknowledged.

"Treehorn," Norma said calmly, too calmly.

"Lower your weapon now or I'll be forced to shoot." He ordered.

Norma lowered her weapon but its barrel stayed pointed in his direction.

"You know I'm here to arrest you." He didn't take his eyes off her.

"Sit down, John. Let's tell a story, you and I, while we wait for the others."

"It's Agent Treehorn," he stated as he kept his rifle aimed at her. He wasn't a rookie and he knew how dangerous a trapped and cornered suspect could become when she had nothing further to lose, her life or her freedom.

Norma pointed her revolver barrel away from Treehorn

but kept her fingers on the grip of the gun as she lowered it to her lap.

The Navajo agent chose the route of his ancestors, offered his respect for an Indian woman, and elder. He pulled his pistol from its holster, aimed it at her, and perched his assault rifle next to hers. He sat cross-legged in front of the fire but maintained the target on her. Samuel and his deputies would arrive in due time to surround them and secure the location.

Norma's voice was calm and conversational. "How does it feel to return home?"

"It felt better leaving than returning," Treehorn derided

"I've watched your career over the years. It's impressive that a half-breed can succeed in a white man's world." Bitterness laced Norma's voice.

"I'm a man of two worlds. That'll never change. My job takes me where there's crime and it doesn't discriminate on skin color," Treehorn's closure rate verified that.

"How do you do it? Day after day, hunting men in the white man's world," She curiously asked.

"I bring closure to the families who've suffered. Bringing the criminal to justice is just one part of my job," the agent replied. "It's never been about their skin color."

"Yes, it is!" Norma spat. "Why is the White Man allowed to come here and victimize us?"

"Crimes go unpunished and that needs to change," Treehorn knew that was once aspect that needed to be addressed.

"And, if they refuse to acknowledge their own behavior like Jason Hodges?"

"It's only a matter of time before justice catches up to them," Treehorn replied honestly, "Or the Creator."

Norma smirked with bitter eyes. "Yes, they do." She examined the Indian petroglyphs that showed horses, rain clouds, and Native American images that graced the ancient weathered rock walls.

"Shadow Dancers tell our story," Norma pointed. "You and I are Shadow Dancers, existing every day as ghosts of ourselves, unable to change our history. We live as empty shells, waiting for the Great Spirit to take us to our loved ones."

"This is true," Treehorn agreed, "Mothers and sons."

"Our spirits live here, both yours and mine. Someone took mine and someone took yours. Hear our song in the wind?" The breeze whistled through the ravine causing the campfire to flare.

Treehorn knew their vision and its revelations, "Tell me our stories," he wisely asked.

Norma added a couple of sticks to the campfire from a pile next to her then she drew a half circle in the sand. "You know I love my horses." It was a statement and not a question. "How hard I worked to breed them," She poked the flames with a stick as if to call a memory, "I was out one morning for my daily ride."

The agent saw the true crime as it unfolded.

"Jason Hodges raised the hood of his truck to signal he's in distress."

Treehorn understood. It's the universal sign of 'help' needed on the Rez.

"When I arrived, he dragged me off my horse and knocked me out with a rock." Norma drew two circles inside her half circle.

Treehorn and Norma both rubbed the scars they carried that their hair concealed.

"When I woke, I'd been stripped of my clothes, and tied to the hood of his car. I was pregnant with a boy. I knew because I had an ultrasound the week before and I begged him not to hurt us." Norma unburdened herself with the horrific events of the day that changed her into a walking ghost. She gripped her gun but didn't point it at him but her fingers clenched it tight as it struck her temple with the butt end. "The baby was a replacement for Noah," she admitted with no shame or guilt.

Treehorn listened and stayed quiet, the Indian way, but kept a tightened grip on his pistol.

"Did you know he's gay?" She asked.

Treehorn shook his head and remained silent.

Norma didn't acknowledge his slight movement, for she was in another world. This was the world where victims lived, the same world Treehorn inhabited.

"Noah refused to give me a grandchild," Norma whispered as she stared unseeing at the canyon walls. "We live our whole lives for no future, nothing?" she asked as her face contorted with the painful memory. She continued her story that the agent needed to hear. "I had to have conjugal visits with Charles in prison to get pregnant," she continued. "How pathetic is that?" Tears streamed down her face. "Jason Hodges hurt me. He was the rock and I became the earth he pulverized. Noah found me here as my dreams bled into the sand." She finished her drawing in the dirt. It was an Indian gravestone marker.

"What happened next?" The timeline emerged.

"Jason Hodges sent me a copy of his book a few months later. He dedicated it to me and my dead baby. He wrote his telephone number inside so I would call him."

Treehorn pictured Norma as she telephoned her rapist. She searched for answers while Jason's patheticness assaulted her call after call. They fed on each other's sickness and despair.

The woman struggled to continue as tears streamed down her face. "I knew the FBI wouldn't arrest him. As you're well aware, very few men are prosecuted on the reservation for sexual assaults. I couldn't report the loss of my baby or the pain I endured. I didn't want my friends to know my shame, or worse, to feel sorry for me."

"You're a victim, Norma. There's no disgrace in that," Treehorn sympathized.

"Why are we treated like dirt?" demanded Norma, as she struck her forehead harder with her gun grip in a useless attempt to erase the nightmare from her mind.

Treehorn knew no amount of pain would succeed, because he'd tried.

Norma confessed, "I called Jason. He laughed. So, I sent Noah to kill him. I told him to make the man suffer and he did. Noah beat him to death, then shoved sand down his throat so his spirit couldn't escape. Jason Hodges killed my son by rape. My son killed Jason Hodges by murder."

Treehorn wondered if confession's good for the soul because as Norma spoke the hostility dissipated from her eyes.

"Tell me about Jeff Hodges," Treehorn requested.

Norma lowered her gun. "Noah and I believed that the Great Spirit had returned Jason Hodges to us. I told Jeff I wouldn't send Noah to kill him this time. I would do it myself. I realized my mistake when he paid with his credit card. He wasn't my rapist, but his identical twin."

"Did he ask Noah for help when he saw him in his uniform?" Treehorn questioned.

"Noah told him he was my son and no one would help him here," Norma stated.

"What happened next?" Treehorn grilled.

"Noah overheard Hodges call the Baltimore police, and

we knew we had to stop him," Norma schemed. "Noah became the willing accomplice, again, for my approval."

"Why involve the boys?" Treehorn suspected her criminal pathology.

"Those rich brats thought they could come to our land and assault our girls like Jason did to me!" Norma spat.

"So, you wanted them to pay?" Treehorn grilled.

"You bet I did. I took from them what Jason took from me, *their souls*. I stole their seed and I bred three girls on the reservation just like my horses. I helped three women whom the land forgot. Those rich lawyers paid well to keep their half-breeds a secret."

The FBI Agent listened as Norma delivered the motive for all of the crimes. "Are there more children?" Treehorn needed to know.

She snorted, "There would have been but a power outage killed the cells in my unit."

"You'll have to answer for your crimes," The agent said

"I lived seventeen years as a ghost of myself. I won't go to prison for it," Norma defended as she raised her revolver and placed Treehorn in its sight. Sneering she asked, "I was here the day my husband killed your wife and when Charles died. Who do you answer to for your crime?"

Navajo Indian Reservation - Antelope Ravine - 15 years earlier

Treehorn sees the white light. The Great Spirit calls him. A gunshot explodes next to him and halts his journey.

Charles, shot in the leg, screams, and flails on the ground.

"John!" Anna whispers to her son, "I'm here." She turns, lifts her rifle, and with all the anger a mother can have on her injured son's behalf, rises and strikes the gunstock against Charles's skull, knocking him unconscious. She rushes to Rocky, removes her Navajo blanket and uses it to cover Skyler, then offers a prayer to the Great Spirit for her. Anna moves and cuts the ropes that bind her son.

The pain and shock keep Treehorn speechless.

Anna helps him put on his pants, binds her son's bleeding wrists, and administers first aid to the cuts on his back. She adds wood to the fire in silence. Her hand grasps her son's and they shuffle their feet and chant in their native tongue. They dance to the rhythms of old and their spirits guide them. Mother and son, Shadow Dancers, highlight the stone wall as their dance ends.

Treehorn regains his strength of life, but not his spirit. He and his mother walk hand-in-hand to Charles's unconscious body.

"You are a man of two lands," Anna says to him. "How do you wish him punished? The way of your Indian mother or your White Man father?"

Treehorn walks to Rocky and removes a pack shovel his mother always carries on her horse. He digs a large hole in the sand. Then he kneels over Charles and packs sand into his mouth. He rolls the body into the hole, face down, and covers it with suffocating sand. He uses the rope that bound his wife and ties it around a flat sandstone boulder. Rocky drags the stone until it covers the grave. Treehorn uses the butt of the rifle and scratches a half circle, two smaller circles, and ten lines into the flat top, creating a gravestone marker.

Norma moved her one hand from her image of a gravestone marker drawn in the sand to caressing the gravestone of her husband next to her. Her finger traced the etching marked on the cold stone. This was the sandstone

Treehorn had engraved there so many years ago. "I was here the day you killed Charles. I watched as you buried him alive beneath this stone," Norma inhaled a deep breath. "I told no one after his death, because you did me a favor."

Treehorn's FBI brain calculated the ramifications of Norma's eyewitness account of the worst day of his life and he felt it, a ghost-like whisper across his body. He needed a distraction. "Noah owns a bullet-proof vest, Norma. He forgave you."

She slowly processed the agent's words, "What? I sh-sh-shot him," she stuttered in disbelief. "He can't survive prison. He can't even die right!" A shocked Norma lowered her weapon. A sad broken woman no longer had her gun aimed at him.

Treehorn looked her over: the witness. Fifteen years he was a widower, fifteen years he was a ghost of himself, and fifteen years he helped victims so he could try to find peace. Today, FBI Special Agent John Treehorn, a Navajo, stopped being a victim. He raised his pistol and shot Norma in the forehead. Her lifeless body fell backward and her blood seeped into the sand next to her husband's gravestone. Their two souls finally reunited in death in their spirit world.

"Justice for you, peace for me," he whispered. His thoughts rose among the spirits in the ravine. Treehorn holstered his weapon and offered a prayer for her soul and his. He added a couple of sticks to the fire and watched them burn while he waited for Samuel and his deputies arrival.

Chapter Thirteen

The FBI, Coroner, and Crime Scene Unit vehicles soon found the isolated location Treehorn had relayed to them when he called in the deaths. Several technicians worked over the area, both inside and outside of the ravine. Treehorn, Samuel, and Raven sat on a couple of boulders at the entrance as the sun rose and watched the proceedings while they drank their coffee. The Police Chief dispatched his deputy's home in the helicopter when they returned Raven to Antelope Ravine. The coroner's staff removed Norma and Noah in matching black-body bags.

"Neither one would've survived prison," Samuel offered his opinion.

"I know," Treehorn nodded and looked at Raven's bandaged arm.

"I'll survive," Raven stated, "the ER stitched it."

Samuel mocked, "Big gun fight, hit with a ricochet."

"Hey, badge of honor," Raven responded.

Samuel and Treehorn chuckled.

The agent focused on the investigation. "What did the

agents recover at Norma's and Noah's houses?"

"Agent Paine found the original towing report for Jeff Hodges' vehicle," Raven replied.

"What was on the DVD?" Treehorn asked specifics.

"Noah made a video of him killing Jason Hodges," Samuel answered. "It was a vicious murder. I didn't think he was capable of such violence."

"I would never have profiled him as being that violent," Raven added.

"He had decades of anger from the way Charles and Norma treated him," Treehorn reflected on how the three of them lived and died in their abusive relationships.

"The men finished their sweep of Norma's properties," continued Raven.

"What did they find at her house?" The Fed asked.

"A copy of the Baltimore DVD and Jason Hodges' book with his telephone number written on the dedication page," Raven supplied.

"The DVD attempted to provide Noah and Norma with justification for their crime." Treehorn needed the details for his report and added, "Anything more?"

"Jeff Hodges' driver's license bookmarked the

dedication page," Raven found the trophy.

"What turned up at the store?"

"The team recovered the blackmail documentation, birth certificates, and all related documents related to the five children," Raven replied. "What happens to them now?"

Treehorn guessed, "A social worker and legal advocate will investigate each of them. They'll make sure they're safe and registered with the tribe."

"Their family," Samuel voiced the irony.

"Yes," Treehorn watched as a staff member approached.

The FBI crime photographer stopped in front of the men. "Can I take a photo?"

The three men nodded and stood up. Treehorn and Raven wore their black FBI-labeled bulletproof vests with their pistols and gold FBI badges attached to their belts. Raven had changed into a clean shirt. "I should show my bandage."

Samuel whispered to Treehorn, "More like, show your stupidity."

Raven heard and chuckled, "I get it, no bandage."

Police Chief Bear stood tall next to the other men in his own black-labeled bulletproof vest and attached gold badge. "Send us all a copy," he requested as the image was taken.

"I will and thanks for the great shot." The photographer smiled and walked away.

"Well, my friends, it's time for me to go home," Treehorn stated as he looked around the home of his birth.

"When do you leave for your white man's world?" Samuel asked.

"Wednesday, but you have my word I'll return soon," Treehorn promised.

"We'll hold you to that!" Raven smiled.

Treehorn and his mother sat in front of the crackling fire and felt its warmth. He put his arm around her and held her tight. "Let me tell you a story," he said. "It all began when an archaeologist came to the reservation." He then described the complete chain of events that ended with the present.

"Jason Hodges was a sick man. He brought his sickness to our land and it spread like a disease," Anna sighed. "Norma's come full circle."

"Hopefully, this will help Edward Hemingford's healing." Treehorn concluded.

"Time will tell," Anna added as she hugged her son.

"This is true," The son whispered as his mother's

unwavering love surrounded him.

Treehorn slept, that night without a nightmare for the first time since his wife's murder.

On the next day, Treehorn accompanied Anna to church and attended a luncheon to reacquaint with old friends and the neighbors he had missed over the years. The day was filled with stories from the past that brought both laughter and regret to Treehorn. He realized he could only blame himself for the time he had spent away from his people, the Diné.

The next day at the Navajo Nation Tribal Orphanage, Treehorn watched from his mother's office as Andy and Sage Foster's arrival.

Anna pointed to the boy and girl in the playroom, "There's Caleb and Callie. Their mother died over a year ago."

Treehorn looked at the pair, "Who took care of them?"

"Their cousins didn't know the identity of the father, so they didn't know who to contact after her death."

The agent watched the two children stack building blocks.

Andy and Sage entered and greeted the agency's social worker.

"Their father's alive," Treehorn added. "They're young and they'll adapt to the changes."

Sage placed a supportive hand on her husband's shoulder as Andy had his first look at his children when the social worker introduced the couple to his twins.

"Your father came through with an emergency temporary custody order," Anna said.

"I know. He emailed me a copy."

"The twins will be raised on the reservation," Anna added.

"It's a good place to grow up," Treehorn offered.

Anna turned to him. "John, I'm sorry."

"Why?" Treehorn asked.

"You didn't have a full-time father." Sadness laced her voice.

"I had you," Treehorn kissed his mother's cheek. "It was enough and I wouldn't change a thing."

"Mother and son," Anna smiled.

Treehorn smiled, "Mother and son."

198

In the afternoon, Treehorn rode Rocky to Skyler's grave site. He swept the dirt off the stone and placed fresh flowers on it. He stood up and spoke to his late wife's spirit. "I have to leave now, but I promise to return soon. I'll miss you." He examined the landscape and saw what he had somehow forgotten during his years away: the beauty of his reservation. "You were right." From somewhere he swore he heard Skyler's whispered reply, 'Justice for you, peace for me.' He kissed his fingertips and placed the kiss on her gravestone. "I promise you, I'll live with that conviction."

He climbed into the saddle on Rocky and shouted, "Let's ride!" And, with those words, horse and rider galloped across the land of his ancestors.

Treehorn arrived early at the FBI office the next morning. He typed his final official report and started on the evidence boxes from the investigation. Each was labeled "Jeff Hodges" with a serialized identification number.

Samuel and Raven drank coffee but wanted beers to celebrate.

"I checked out Andy Foster's hit-and-run," Samuel said.

"What did you find?" The agent asked as he filled the boxes.

"Norma Begay's car insurance company verified that sh had filed a claim a few days after the accident. The damage was on the right front fender," Samuel stated.

Raven glanced at the financial documents. "Why did Norma blackmail Andy Foster so many years later?"

"I examined her bank records. She needed the money. When Andy's grandfather refused to pay money for the blackmail video, they didn't want the exposure. The lawyers were willing to pay for their silence. Norma made a mistake when the twins' DNA didn't match the lawyer's DNA. Since the grandfather refused to pay for the video, we'll never know what transpired between Andy's grandfather and Norma. We can only assume Andy was struck in retaliation. Since they'r both dead, we'll never have the definitive answer," Treehorn stated as he continued to fill the evidence box to the top with documents.

Raven removed Edward's chest-carving image from the bulletin board. "Why would Edward draw a burial marker on his chest?" Raven asked. "He didn't kill anyone or bury a body."

Treehorn knew, "It's not a gravestone marker."

"What is it?" Raven asked.

Examining the image, Treehorn pictured himself in Edward's position in the vehicle on the night of the boy's assault. "Edward was in the rear seat facing forward. Jeff Hodges handcuffed to the front seat facing him. The drawing is Jeff's bloodied face, his eyes, and his ten fingers handcuffed to the head rest. It's what Edward remembered from that night."

Raven nodded. "Watching Jeff Hodges as he suffered in the front seat traumatized him for fifteen years."

"Why kill Jeff Hodges?" Samuel asked.

"Jeff represented everything opposite from Norma's and Noah's life. He was a loving father who tried to protect the boys in his care. All we can assume is that Norma and Noah dropped the boys off at the highway, then they drove to Antelope Ravine where they tortured Jeff and placed his body beneath the hood. We'll never know what happened that night. All we know is Noah admitted to killing him for Norma. I'll assume they didn't want a witness to their crimes. The boys were drugged and their heads covered. They couldn't identify either Noah or Norma, only the images as Shadow Dancers."

"I wonder if Jeff knew that his death was caused by his brother's crime," Raven reflected.

"Only the Great Spirit knows." Samuel surmised.

Treehorn suspected Norma informed the twin brother before his death. He placed the remaining documents into the evidence box and closed its cover. He'd bet money on his badge that Jeff was aware of Jason's aberrant behavior and that's why the twins lacked a close relationship.

Samuel handed his friend a beer. "We can have one. Congratulations! Another case solved."

Treehorn chugged his drink.

"Number fifty-seven as lead investigator. I called your office to verify your count."

The three men raised their beers, "To justice!" Treehorn declared.

"To justice," Samuel and Raven concurred.

They bumped their bottles together and celebrated.

Later, in the quiet security vault, the agent solemnly filed the evidence boxes next to the other crime files. Jason and Jeff Hodges' cases were officially closed and Treehorn hoped that Norma and Noah were at peace.

Chapter Fourteen

Meanwhile, in Washington, Leo Mancuso signed the closure paperwork on the investigation he'd received from Treehorn. He opened his wall safe and removed a cream vellum business card that held a single telephone number on it. Not printed in gold ink, but in actual gold. Mancuso dialed the number and the telephone rang. No one answered today.

In the morning, Raven handed Treehorn a copy of the local Indian Times newspaper as he exited the FBI office with his luggage and briefcase. It's photograph taken outside of Antelope Ravine and the headline read: *FBI and Navajo Nation Police Solve Cold Case Murder*. The photo showed the three officers dressed in their black gear with their gold badges. He shoved it inside his luggage and placed his bags into the SUV. He'd examine it on the plane. Samuel, Raven, Mary, and Anna were there to send him off.

Samuel shook Treehorn's hand. "Come back real soon," he smiled.

"I will," Treehorn replied and knew he would.

Mary stepped forward, handed Treehorn a little box, and kissed his cheek. "Here are some goodies for your trip."

Treehorn kissed hers. "Thank you. I miss you already!" Mary turned away before she started to bawl.

Anna's turn. She hugged and kissed her son. She whispered in his ear, "I'll plant some flowers on Skyler's hill."

Treehorn gave his mother a comforting hug and whispered, "She'd like that."

Anna released her son with the regret only a mother felt "I'll visit you real soon in Washington."

"I'd like that," Treehorn smiled.

Raven had stood by, watching the others. He shook Treehorn's hand, "Thanks for solving my case."

Treehorn's laughed. They smiled and their spirits soared because it was the first time they heard him laugh in years.

"Any time, pissant," Treehorn replied.

Raven and the others laughed. The two continued their banter as they traveled to the airport.

A few days later a FedEx van arrived at Cynthia Hodges house. The driver knocked on her door to deliver an envelope "Are you Cynthia Hodges?" he asked.

"Yes?" She wasn't expecting anything.

He proffered the electronic tablet. "Sign on the X, please."

Cynthia signed while he scanned the envelope. "Thanks." She examined the envelope address. She slit it open and removed a check for three million dollars from her deceased husband's life insurance company. The widow promptly burst into tears.

At the Baltimore Homicide Division, a staff member delivered a package from the FBI to Detective Williams. He opened the envelope and removed a DVD labeled 'Jason Hodges - Homicide' and a Certificate of Merit from the FBI for the detective's help in solving the murder of Jason Hodges. He shouted, "Thank you, Agent Treehorn!"

The agent secured his weapon in a locker at the Bellingham Psychiatric Hospital. A nurse escorted him to the activity room where he found Eliza and Edward Hemingford drinking tea. Treehorn shook Eliza's hand and her son's as he introduced himself, "Hello, Edward. My name is John Treehorn."

"It's nice that you've come to visit," she greeted.

"Do I know you?" asked Edward as his eyes focused on the visitor.

Treehorn looked at the young man with the clean-cut hair and newly trimmed beard. "I'm an FBI Special Agent. I lead an investigation of a missing person on the Navajo India Reservation. I'm here to tell you and your mother about a chain of events that occurred many years ago. It's about a bo who once thought a horrible crime had been committed against him, but in fact, it hadn't. He's the lucky one."

The staff and patients went about their activities on the psychiatric ward as Treehorn told a Shadow Dancer's story.

The End

STOLEN SISTERS A John Treehorn Mystery (Book 2) FBI Special Agent John Treehorn hunts a killer in an oil field boom town where several indigenous women have gone missing or murdered.

BAD PENNY A John Treehorn Mystery (Short Read #1) FBI Special Agent John Treehorn hunts for the killer of an Indian Posse member. Two Indians are found with the murder weapon and neither one chooses to confess. (All royalties go to charity.)

INDIAN POSSE A John Treehorn Mystery (Book 3) FBI Special Agent John Treehorn hunts for the killer of two Indian Posse members, a vicious gang who hunts criminals who haven't paid their debts to society.

Please join the author page to keep posted on future Treehorn novels and short reads:
https://www.facebook.com/SpecialAgentJohnTreehorn/

www.dinahmiller.com (Books, merchandise, and mugs.)

Thank You.

Made in United States
North Haven, CT
26 August 2023

40740747R00129